This Book Belongs To:

....

....

Soaring above the Clouds

An Autobiography of Perseverance and Victory

Deborah-May Coetzee

First published in 2019
Second Edition published in 2021 by
Honeybee Publications

Paperback: 978-1-80227-257-4
eBook: 978-1-80227-258-1

While every effort has been made to ensure the information published in this book is accurate, the author, editors, publisher and printers take no responsibility for any loss or damages suffered by any person as a result of reliance upon the information contained herein. The publisher respectfully advises readers to obtain professional advice concerning the content.

AUTHOR DEBORAH-MAY COETZEE
Email: soaringabovethecloudsbio@gmail.com
Website: www.deborah-mayauthor.com

Scripture quotations taken from the HOLY BIBLE, NEW INTERNATIONAL VERSION. Copyright © 1973, 1978, 1984 by International Bible Society. Used by permission.

Dedication

This book is firstly dedicated to my Heavenly Father without whom nothing is possible, not even the air that I breathe! He has made a way where there seemed to be no way. He has given fulfilment, joy and purpose to life in spite of bleak hopelessness. Without my Heavenly Father, I am nothing.

Secondly, this book is dedicated to my father who is in heaven, Walter Albert Coetzee. Born 2nd of September 1952 and went home to be with the Lord on the 1st of September 2015. Dad never treated me as a person with a disability and I am where I am because of it.

Blessings from Debs

Contents

Acknowledgements

Writing a book about the story of my life has been a surreal process. There were times when I thought this project was simply a pipe dream. If it were not for the gentle, constant prompting of my Lord and Saviour, this project would never have come to fruition. He has given me such a fulfilled lifestyle despite an absolute hopeless diagnosis, that there is no way that I could not share it with the world.

I'm forever indebted to my very good friends, Brendon and Belinda Buckland and Marius and Debra Marais for their editorial help, keen insight, and ongoing support in bringing my story to life. It is because of their efforts and encouragement that this book has been published.

The back cover pictures of this book each have a very personal meaning as they were taken on trips to the Kruger National Park of which I was privileged to be a part. These photos (including my personal photo) were taken by Shirley Mitchell. Shirley has been a very dear friend to me for over two decades. Shirley and I have a motto - *"What happens in the Park stays in the Park"* and this motto holds many funny, fond memories.

The photo on the signature page (first page) was taken by Meg Coates Palgrave, a friend & renowned tree expert, also on one of our thrilling trips to the Kruger National Park. Meg, it is a privilege for me to use this photo!

The people mentioned in this book have played a vital role in how my life story has panned out and I want to thank each and every one for the input that you have had. However, there are so many others who have not been mentioned in this book; you know who you are and I want you to know that the roles you have played and still play in my life are invaluable.

Finally, I am extremely thankful for the love and encouragement of my family!

I love and appreciate you all!

Foreword

I met Debbie in 2004 when we moved to Polokwane. Debbie soon became my best friend, and although we only lived there for three and a half years, she will be my best friend for as long as I live. Other than my husband, I don't think there is anyone who will ever know me as well as she does. She not only taught me so much about what it's like to live with a disability, she also taught me so much about myself.

I will never forget the evening that we met. She looked as though she needed help with something and I offered to help. She looked at me and said, "Do I look like a cripple?" I was in shock. How do I reply to that? She clearly is disabled, but it would be terribly rude to say "yes". She soon started laughing and even though I can't remember if she actually needed help at that time or not, I will never forget the impact she has had on my life. That evening was the beginning of the journey.

Debbie taught me to laugh; most importantly, to laugh at myself. She was very gentle with me and the teasing started so softly. She knew me well and knew exactly what I could handle. Through this learning, she was such an example to me. If she could laugh about some of her weaknesses and struggles, I surely could too. Debbie had learnt to accept how God had created her, and this was a lesson I desperately needed to learn for myself.

Debbie also taught me what it truly means to trust God. I remember a discussion we once had about healing. She told me that if God had to come and offered to completely restore her physically – she would probably have to say "no thanks." The reason? She didn't want to lose the relationship she had with Him. She has to rely on God each day for so many tasks we "normal people" just take for granted; getting dressed, making breakfast or even just getting somewhere other that home. Trust is not just something she has in her mind. It is needed for her daily life. Now, over ten years since leaving South

Africa, I have a six-year-old daughter with disabilities. Although the situation is different to Debbie's, I know that the lessons I learnt from her have been instrumental in helping me to trust God through these very hard years.

I thank the Lord for Debbie and the impact she has had on my life. So, I am thrilled to recommend this book to you. How exciting that you can get to know Debbie as she shares with you the journey that she has been on. How wonderful that you get to learn and grow and be encouraged by her life too.

— Belinda Buckland, author of *God's Book of Wisdom*

Epilogue:
Ruffled Feathers

The alarm goes off at 04:45. I awake with another migraine, caused by muscle spasms. Today is really bad and the normal everyday experience of muscular pain fades in comparison to the throbbing of my head. I feel nauseous. I tell myself that I still have one hour and fifteen minutes before I REALLY have to get up; perhaps by then, the blinding pain would have eased.

It is a busy time of the year at work and I don't want to take the day off.

The clock reaches 06:00 all too quickly and I pray for the strength to get up, get ready and be at work by 07:00. My head is still throbbing, causing my muscles to painfully tense up even more, making it harder than usual to dress myself. I am so grateful that I can at least use one arm, although due to overuse, my tendonitis has flared up, making any movement of the arm extremely painful. I am finally dressed, with time to spare to make myself a cup of coffee. It is difficult to lift my arm even slightly, but as I remove the milk from the fridge, as always, I pray for strength. I receive the strength to safely pour the boiling water. My nice, hot cup of coffee is finally made but with one uncontrolled spastic movement, I knock the cup over. Coffee is everywhere and as I make a feeble attempt at cleaning it up, tears of pain, frustration and despair roll down my cheeks.

My helper, Rahab, arrives to assist with a couple of things before pushing me to work in the wheelchair. Rahab quickly takes over and cleans up the rest of the coffee. My head is still throbbing, my precious arm is still so painful and I wonder how I am going to manage work today.

I battle to pick up and hand over some change to a customer who has bought a school uniform for his child. He can't understand how somebody with such limitations could be employed in my position and he unkindly verbalises his thoughts. I pray for strength not to retaliate but to keep trusting that this unusually intense pain is only for a season. The phone rings, I answer, but the person on the other end cannot understand my slurred speech and simply puts the phone down on me. I console myself with the thought that at least this time I was not accused of being a drunkard! Fortunately, Rahab is there to assist me with most of the physical work today. Hannie, a colleague and good friend, straps my arm in a sling and once again I receive the strength to swing my arm over the keyboard and hit the keys, ensuring that my work for the day is done despite the excruciating pain.

Against Rahab's protests, I go to Bible study in the evening. My headache has eased a bit, but my arm is still in a sling. I am not sure if it is the way I am sitting or the way the sling is fastened, but a while into the Bible study, my arm starts throbbing; deeper into the Bible study, the pain becomes unbearable and I am desperate for the session to come to a close. Also attending the Bible study are two doctors and a therapist, all three of whom work together. Liz, one of the doctors and the therapist are good friends of mine, but the other doctor is only visiting tonight. Upon realising the intensity of my pain, they make the decision to bundle me into their car and take me to the hospital where they live and work and give me treatment for the pain. All my muscles are in spasm now and as I try to stand up, my left knee gives in and I fall back down into the chair. Apparently, the pain in my knee is called *referred pain* and is a result of the intense pain in my arm. Finally, I reach the car, short of being carried. By now, I have broken out in a cold sweat and once in the car, my legs are rigidly splayed out in front of me in spasm. When we get to the hospital, Liz gives me strong painkillers and within a few minutes, the pain starts easing and I begin to relax. The three ladies very kindly take me home and help me into bed, and the pain is now more bearable. I know those three ladies had not been at Bible study that night by chance!!!

I thank God for helping me through today as He has done so many days in the past and ask Him to give me His strength to overcome the hurdles of tomorrow.

As I face daily challenges of various kinds, I enjoy an independent lifestyle, totally dependent on His strength to get me through each day!

Welcome to my exciting world!

Introduction:
Thorny Nest

"In a desert land he found him, in a barren and howling waste.

He shielded him and cared for him; he guarded him as the apple of his eye, like an eagle that stirs up its nest and hovers over its young, that spreads its wings to catch them and carries them aloft."

— Deuteronomy 32:10-11

I have often heard it being illustrated that as a mother fish eagle builds her nest, thorns and briars are what make up a big part of her nesting material! When the eaglets are old enough to start learning to fly, the mother will carry them on her pinions high up into the air and then drop them. As the eaglets fall towards the ground, some will quickly catch on to the art of flying but the mother eagle will swoop down under those little ones who are slow to learn and carry them on her wings back to the safety of their nest. However, once the ever-growing eaglets are back in their nest, the discomfort caused by the thorns and briars which have been built into their nest will cause them to long for their independence, causing them to try harder at acquiring their survival skills.

Our trials also play an important role in our lives here on earth. Through our trials, we learn to exercise and strengthen our muscles of faith and in many aspects, they prepare us for the various ways in which God wants to use us in service to Him. *"Consider it pure joy, my brothers, whenever you face trials of many kinds, because you know that the testing of your faith develops perseverance. Perseverance must finish its work so that you may be mature and complete, not lacking anything."* James 1:2-4

Contrary to the popular teaching that it is always God's will for us to be healed, it is my prayer that whoever reads this book will be encouraged to learn that there truly is great power in our weaknesses. Not for one moment do I doubt that God could heal me in an instant. He doesn't even need my faith to do so. However, up until this point, He has not done so, choosing to use my disability to impact lives in a far greater way than an actual physical healing could ever have been used. I can truly say that choosing to use my weaknesses for His glory is an absolute honour for me as I have come to know Him in ways that I am sure I would never have known Him if I was not forced to be so dependent on Him.

"My grace is sufficient for you, for my power is made perfect in weakness. Therefore I will boast all the more gladly about my weaknesses, so that Christ's power may rest on me."

— 2 Corinthians 12:8-10

Chapter One:
A Little Egg Is Hatched

"For You formed my inward parts; You wove me in my mother's womb."

— Psalm 139:13

African Fish Eagles are known to be monogamous, breeding once a year. Typical of eagles, their nests are reused every season, growing with the addition of new material each year. The breeding display consists of much soaring and calling with very occasional claw-grappling. One to three white eggs are laid at three-day intervals.

The journey begins

As a teenager and one of Elvis Presley's most devoted fans, my mother would sit with her school friends doting over their Rock 'n Roll hero. My mother would jokingly say that one day when she married, her child would be born on January the 8th (Elvis' birthday).

My parents were married in 1973. My dad was extremely handsome and had lamb chop side burns just like Elvis. My mum was tall, slim and very pretty. They had been dating for some time when my dad proposed to my mum in the most romantic way imaginable: at a traffic light, just before the light turned green!

My parents lived in Rhodesia and were not among the wealthiest. As with

1

most newlyweds, they struggled financially. Dad worked as a farmer and Mum worked as an office clerk. Though money was very scarce, they were very happy together and eagerly awaited the birth of their first child.

My mother had an uncomplicated pregnancy and though not all the necessary tests had been performed throughout her pregnancy, by today's standards, everything seemed to be going well.

Their first little fledgling made her entrance into the world at around 07:00 a on January the 8th 1974. The birth was not without complication. My mother had woken with contractions and my father had rushed her to hospital. They were made to sit on a hard bench and fill out forms, by which time the contractions were not far apart. At last, a stern-looking nursing sister fetched my mother and prepared her for the delivery. Finally, the doctor arrived, but according to Mum, he treated her very roughly. Upon observing the rough treatment of the doctor, the Sister tried to comfort my mum and encourage her by telling her that she was doing "just fine".

At birth, the baby girl was having trouble breathing and was very stressed. She was quickly taken away and a paediatrician was called in to perform a lumbar puncture in order to find out what was upsetting her.

My mum only got the chance to hold me for the first time a couple of days later, after I had been in the incubator. Breastfeeding was almost an impossible task as I was not sucking very well, and as a result, I had to go onto a bottle.

My parents lived in a little one-bedroom flat, and so I slept in their room in my pram. It was very hard to feed me and due to the fact that I was not sucking very well and not getting enough milk, I would constantly cry. This was very stressful for my mum. She was a new mother and often wondered what she was doing wrong.

There were many nights where my constant crying just didn't stop. Mum would sit up in the lounge with me the whole night so that Dad could get a bit of sleep. She would fall asleep in the early hours of the morning, awaking when she heard the milkman at the door. Often on Sundays, during our usual Sunday lunches with my grandmother, Mum would fall asleep at the table. Gran would step in and try her utmost to bottle feed me.

One night, at three weeks old, my unusual crying started once again. Seeing Mum's despair, my dad gave me a pat on the bum, turned me over in my pram and I fell asleep. This time it worked. They didn't know what was wrong and worry was consuming them.

My parents were never informed of the outcome of the tests though they had suspicions that something was wrong because my paediatrician insisted on seeing me every month. During these visits, I would be weighed, various exercises with my limbs were attempted and even more tests were performed, but still nothing was mentioned to my parents about my condition. During one visit the paediatrician requested X-rays. For the X- rays, the nurses needed my arms raised above my head. Because of my condition, this was impossible and so the nurses tried to force my arms up, causing me to cry out in pain and fear. Like an avenging angel, my mum snatched me up and took me home.

Much to my parents' distress, my mother was forced to return to work when I was two weeks old. My auntie Caroline and her mother looked after me during the day. Having to leave me and return to work was very upsetting for my parents, especially since they were aware of the fact that something was wrong but didn't know exactly what.

According to my aunt, I was a pleasure to look after. I enjoyed my bath and my behaviour patterns were as normal as all the other babies which her family had looked after. They, therefore, had no suspicion that anything was amiss.

To compound matters, Dad would be away from home for periods as long as six weeks at a time, due to his serving in the Rhodesian army during the Rhodesian Bush War from 1969 until 1980.

This was an extremely difficult time for the whole country. Wives and children left behind were never sure if their loved ones would return home, while those who had left to serve in the army were never certain of the safety of the loved ones they had left behind. Thankfully, Dad always came home, though scars left by what he had seen and experienced never quite left him. One of my uncles had his leg shot up and another uncle was involved in a landmine explosion. Thankfully, both survived.

Final diagnoses

Finally, after 18 months of turmoil, the doctors could answer some of my parents' questions. Whether they could only make a proper diagnosis after 18 months, or only then gathered enough courage to tell my parents, the truth is unknown. My parents' reaction was of total despair and anguish. I can't imagine the agony, the guilt and the anger that accompanied the little relief that such a diagnosis brought them after such prolonged uncertainty.

I was diagnosed with severe Cerebral Palsy (CP). My family was not familiar with CP and desperately searched for possible cures for this condition. My grandfather was even prepared to send me overseas and pay for operations which he thought would cure me.

My family was even more distraught when they were sadly informed that no operation which may help my condition existed.

From the age of twenty months, I began attending St Giles Rehabilitation Centre in Rhodesia, now known as Zimbabwe.

The following is a Nursery report written when I was twenty-two months old:

Nursery

Deborah was admitted to the Nursery on 16th September 1975. At first, she screamed most of the morning unless handled by an African assistant. She was still on a bottle, could not sit unsupported, would not attempt to play with toys.

She was happy at lunchtime but cried when put down for a rest afterwards. She can roll and can crawl when supported under the stomach by a towel, and can kneel holding on to the side of the cot. She can pick up small bricks, has finger and thumb coordination with her left hand but tends to leave her right hand out of all activities. She drinks from a cup but cannot hold it properly and can feed herself fairly well. She will sit on the potty but very rarely uses it. She doesn't like strangers and gets upset if picked up. She has temper tantrums and will scream for long periods if she cannot get her way. Deborah takes interest in her surroundings and enjoys the company of the older children in the afternoons. Deborah settled very slowly to the nursery routine and surroundings but now appears to be making good progress.

Medical Impression

Deborah is a cerebral palsied child primarily with a right hemiplegia but with some spasticity on the left side.

Recommendations

Deborah is functioning below her chronological age in all areas. We would like Deborah to remain at St. Giles where she will receive the necessary stimulation of the nursery and physiotherapy.

Assessment Report by St. Giles Rehabilitation Centre – 26th November 1975.

At St. Giles, I received intense therapy such as physical, occupational and speech therapy. As a baby and young child, these sessions often resulted in tears brought on by pain and frustration.

While still in the Rehabilitation nursery, I was unable to sit independently and had to sit in a special half-circular cushion as I could not support myself and would flop to the side when unaided. My neck muscles were not strong enough to support my head, which would loll to the side.

Therapy was intense and progress was slow. Due to the fact that doctors had predicted that I would never walk, my physical therapists focused on trying to get me mobile, at least to the point of crawling, but I first had to learn how to roll over on my own, which also helped strengthen my neck muscles. Once this was achieved, the next step was learning how to crawl properly, but this part of therapy proved extremely difficult. I was accustomed to getting around by "bunny-hopping". This method was bad for the further development of my muscles and changing the way I got around was important but terribly difficult and painful. However, after much exercise, correct crawling was achieved.

When I was a bit older, my therapist then decided to try and get me even more mobile by trying to teach me to ride a tricycle. I was excited at the thought that I would be able to get around more. However, this proved to be very hard work and even after strapping my feet to the pedals with bandages, this endeavour proved impossible.

In the meantime, I wore calipers and built-up boots during the day. It took time to become accustomed to the calipers and boots as they were designed to try and stretch my legs and help change the pattern of my in-turned feet.

When I reached preschool age, I was made to stand in a special standing box. It had a table on which I did my school work for certain periods of time each day.

Occupational therapy was focused on teaching me to do things on my own such as dressing myself, feeding myself and at the early age of five, I began typing on an electric typewriter with the aid of a key guard.

Speech therapy was centred around trying to obtain formation of words and then a clearer pronunciation of words. Later, this included breathing exercises, which made a huge difference to the clarity of my speech.

My mother was given physical exercises to do with me during school holidays.

As a baby and young child, I experienced convulsions. These were brought on by great excitement or trauma. As a result, the family tried to control excitement by trying not to make too much of a big deal of Christmas or birthdays. They also tried to ease the intensity of upsets such as the death of a loved one or a pet. I was also given medication to control these convulsions. The medication had many side effects, including being the cause of constant, severe mouth ulcers. I was on the medication for twenty-five years.

Although there are still many questions surrounding the cause of my CP, what a waste of precious moments it would be if I were to dwell on the "what ifs" of over four decades ago. Life goes on and by God's grace, every opportunity that comes our way needs to be snatched up and used to its fullest. Dwelling on the "what ifs" of yesterday only leads to despair and robs one of the joy of victoriously living today and every day hereafter.

In the chapters to follow, it is my most sincere desire that you, dear reader, will be greatly encouraged as you read about the personal hurdles that I have faced and how they have been victoriously overcome by a Power which is so much greater than anything we could ever imagine.

Psalm 139 verse 16b gives us insight into the comfort, joy and victory that we can experience in the midst of our everyday trials: *"And in Your book were all written the days that were ordained for me, when as yet there was not one of them."*

What is cerebral palsy?

Cerebral palsy is a term used to describe a group of chronic conditions affecting body movements and muscle coordination. It is caused by damage to one or more specific areas of the brain, usually occurring during fetal development, or during infancy. It can also occur before, during or shortly following birth.

"Cerebral" refers to the brain and "Palsy" to a disorder of movement or posture. If someone has cerebral palsy, it means that because of an injury to their brain (cerebral), they are not able to use some of the muscles in their body in the normal way (palsy). Children with cerebral palsy may not be able to walk, talk, eat or play in the same ways as most other children.

Cerebral palsy is neither progressive nor communicable. It is also not "curable" in the accepted sense, although education, therapy and applied technology can help persons with cerebral palsy lead productive lives. It is important to know that cerebral palsy is not a disease or illness. It isn't contagious and it doesn't get worse. Children who have cerebral palsy will have it all their lives.

Cerebral palsy is characterised by an inability to fully control motor function, particularly muscle control and coordination. Depending on which areas of the brain have been damaged, one or more of the following may occur:

- muscle tightness or spasm
- involuntary movement
- disturbance in gait and mobility
- abnormal sensation and perception
- impairment of sight, hearing or speech
- seizures

There are three main types of cerebral palsy:

- Spastic Cerebral Palsy (stiff and difficult movement)
- Athetoid Cerebral Palsy (involuntary and uncontrolled movement)
- Ataxic Cerebral Palsy (disturbed sense of balance and depth perception)
- Mixed Cerebral Palsy

There may be a combination of these types for any one person.

Internet. about-cerebral-palsy.org – Google: Definition of Cerebral Palsy

My cerebral palsy is a combination of all three types. The doctors guessed (probably in an attempt to answer some of my parents' many questions) that the brain damage was caused by the birth process that had taken place too quickly.

Chapter Two:
Secure Under the Feathers

"For this reason I say to you, do not be worried about your life, as to what you will eat or what you will drink; nor for your body, as to what you will put on. Is not life more than food, and the body more than clothing? "Look at the birds of the air, that they do not sow, nor reap nor gather into barns, and yet your heavenly Father feeds them. Are you not worth much more than they?"

— Matthew 6:25-26

Usually, it is the mother eagle who patiently feeds each chick, gently coaxing it to take a shred of meat from her fiercely hooked beak. Over and over, she offers food, eating rejected morsels herself, and then tearing off a fresh piece, she tries again. Both parents use their bodies to protect the chicks from the elements, sitting dutifully on their nests during the baking sun or drenching rain.

Close calls

My third year was an eventful one and God's hand of protection was experienced very tangibly on two occasions.

In celebration of my third birthday, my parents took me along with them to the "drive-in" to watch a movie. On our way home, I was sitting in the front seat on Mum's lap. These were the days before the law was so strict regarding seatbelts and toddler car seats. As any tired toddler, I became restless and Mum put me onto the back seat. Literally minutes after putting me in the back, another vehicle skipped a traffic light and collided into our vehicle. Mum went through the windscreen and landed on the tarmac. Apart from other multiple injuries, Mum's left cheek had to be stitched back onto her face. She had forty-eight stitches in her face. Dad also sustained light injuries. Although very shaken, I got away with just a couple of scratches and bruises. If I had still been on my mother's lap at the time of the accident, I would have been killed.

On the second occasion, because we were living in a malaria-infested area, Mum one day asked the doctor for anti-malaria pills for the family. I was three and a half years old. The doctor took a bottle of pills from his dispensary. The bottle indicated clearly that it was not to be given to children. However, he instructed Mum to give me half a tablet that night, before I went to bed. Mum forgot and though Dad suggested that she wake me and give me the medication, they decided to give it to me in the morning. I was given the medication in the morning before being dropped off at St Giles nursery.   It was while we were being given breakfast that one of the helpers noticed that my lips, fingernails and toenails had turned blue and that I was not breathing. I was given oxygen and rushed to the hospital, where I stayed for two days while doctors tried to flush the drug out of my system. If Mum had given me the medication the night before, they would have woken the next morning to a lifeless child.

Determined to beat the odds

From a very young age, I was convinced that I would one day walk. However, doctors strongly advised my parents not to encourage this expectation because they were convinced that I would hardly ever be able to do anything for myself, let alone walk.   They were concerned that the disappointment brought on by the harsh realisation that I would indeed never walk, would intensify my convulsions.

Nevertheless, my parents chose not to heed this advice and always encouraged me not to give up trying to walk.

The blessing of a sibling

On the 6th of November 1978, I became a very proud sister to my baby brother, Cristo. Mum had complications while giving birth to Cristo and it was discovered that the umbilical cord was wrapped around his neck. Thankfully, this major complication was detected in time, Mum was given an emergency Caesarean and a healthy baby was delivered. My parents were told that if the complication had not been detected in time, Cristo could also have been brain-damaged.

I was treated no differently from other children and received my fair share of discipline. I was also very proud of my baby brother. So, my parents realized that the punishment of not being able to hold my baby brother proved much more effective than any other kind of punishment I received for bad behaviour.

Glimmer of hope

At age five, progress became very apparent; the following is an academic report written at 5 years and 6 months:

Academic Testing

Debbie is a bright little girl, very alert and very energetic. Her grouping, matching and sequencing are all very good. Although she is only 5 years old, I felt she was ready to start formal school work this term. She can read and type her numbers to ten and she can do addition and subtraction using the sticking method. She can read the names of colours and she has started reading books from the Ladybird Reading Scheme. She has a good memory and appears to retain everything learnt. She has learnt to use an electric typewriter with a grid over the keys and types her name and numbers. As she progresses with her formal school work, she will use the typewriter more frequently. She is happy and talkative and keen to participate in all activities. She works to the best of her ability and is obtaining good results.

Assessment Report by St. Giles Rehabilitation Centre – July 1979

The power of prayer

Around the age of seven, my parents began taking me to see a lady by the name of Barbara. We would go and see Barbara almost every Sunday for about a year. Barbara and her husband, Bill, were a very loving couple and they made it their mission to intercede for me throughout the week and on Sundays. When I would go and see them, they would lay hands on me and faithfully pray for me. It was not long after, much to everyone's joy, that I started standing. I started standing unaided at age eight.

The odds beaten

Though my legs were very rigid and weak, I was hard-headed and stubborn. I was determined to walk. As a young child, I would push myself up against the couch into a standing position and then slowly try and take a few steps towards the coffee table (which was only a couple of feet away) and then I would flop backwards back onto the couch.

At age ten, I joined a group of children from the school who went horse-riding every Friday morning. I was excited, as I love animals, but my very first time on a horse was a very scary experience. I was lifted up onto the horse, with a helper on both sides holding my feet, and a third helper in front, leading the horse. Though nervous, I soon began to relax and enjoy the ride. Horse-riding is a wonderful form of therapy. Not only is the interaction with the animal very therapeutic, but while riding the horse, the rhythm of the horse helps to relax the muscles and to improve balance and coordination.

Horse-riding also helps to stretch the muscles and strengthen muscle tone and it was only after a few months of riding that I took my first independent, unaided steps.

My mother and grandmother were called in by my physical therapist one morning and they were overcome with joy as they watched me take a few shaky, independent steps towards them – *I could indeed walk by myself!*

Now I knew for sure that I would soon be walking independently, but this meant much more painful physical therapy. My boots were built up even more and much time was spent on trying to develop my walking pattern. In the beginning, I experienced many serious falls, often landing on my head and yet I marvel at how I have, to date, never been injured too seriously. Over time, I became steadier on my feet.

As an adult, though my walking pattern is very unique and I still experience falls, I praise God with all my heart that I can walk unaided for fair distances.

Early years in boarding school

My parents moved onto a plot out of town and decided that putting me in boarding school would be in my best interest. I was eight years old when I first started boarding school at St Giles Rehabilitation Centre. Though I went home regularly, especially during the first few years of boarding school, for the duration of our time in Zimbabwe I never really settled down properly.

Some of my earliest memories of boarding school are of the fire drills which often took place during the early 1980s. The bush war had recently come to an end, but regular drills continued as a precaution. Often these drills would take place in the middle of the night. Everyone had to be outside in the courtyard for roll call within five minutes after the shrill of the siren. Those of us who were unable to walk had to ensure that we got out there, even if it meant crawling over the rough tarmac. Only those who were incapable of manoeuvering themselves at all were carried out and laid on the tarmac until after roll call.

Overall, boarding school proved to be of great benefit to me. I was strongly encouraged to try and do more things for myself. With good discipline from the hostel staff, I slowly began to improve in all areas, including dressing myself. However, feeding myself, even at age eight, proved to be a very messy affair and I would happily have preferred to have someone else feed me!

Faithful service

My parents employed various helpers over the years to assist with my care when I went home for weekends and school holidays. While I was at school, they would assist Mum with the housework but none of these helpers would match up to the faithfulness of Annie. Annie worked for the family for over ten years. She loved it when Cristo and I came home for the holidays, even though it meant more work for her. Annie loved taking Cristo and myself for long walks, regardless of her other responsibilities around the house. Annie would become very upset when either of us was disciplined and often tried to protect us from it, even though she knew that the discipline was for our own good. She hated seeing me sick or in pain and when I became ill or experienced a break out of boils (as I often did in my early teenage years), she would do almost anything to try and ease the pain, even if it meant advising Mum with her own traditional remedies.

It was during my bath times that Annie would patiently teach me how to speak her home language, Shona. In time, Shona became my second language; I could speak it fluently and this ability would prove to be of great benefit to me as I grew up in an environment that was made up predominantly of Shona-speaking people.

First healing service

In the -mid-nineteen eighties, the whole city of Harare was abuzz with the news

14

of an upcoming international healing crusade. Posters guaranteeing healing to all lame and sick were hanging from virtually every lamp post in town. Request boxes had also been placed in various parts of town, in which people could deposit their healing requests. This was big news at the school and those who had the slightest bit of faith wrote or had someone else write their healing requests on pieces of paper and gave them to a staff member, who deposited them into a request box in town for us. I didn't *think* that I would be healed. I *knew* that I would be healed. There was just no doubt in my mind. I believed in miracles and I believed that nothing would stop God from healing this ten-year-old cerebral palsied little girl. The build-up to the healing service was filled with great anticipation. Two friends and I counted down the days leading up to the service. The day we had been waiting so long for finally arrived, and, as our wheelchairs were being loaded into the bus, we visualised ourselves returning to the hostel without them. Despite our excitement, the service seemed really short and before we knew it, we were being loaded back into the bus, still in our wheelchairs! Stunned and dismayed, I asked one of the workers from the crusade, who was helping us into the bus, why we were leaving so early? And why we were missing the healing part of the service? Why had we not been called up onto the stage? And why had nobody come to pray for us? He answered that the service was over and that it was time for everyone to go home. The let-down was just too overwhelming. We had believed with all our hearts that we would be healed that day and no one had even come to pray for us. This experience left a deep impression on me and had the potential to do great harm with regard to any relationship that I could have with the Church in the future.

Cause for concern

At age eleven, my convulsions seemed unusually more frequent. The following is an abstract from a hostel report written in February 1985:

Hostel report

Last December holiday, Debbie was with her parents, but she did not have a good holiday; she had three epileptic attacks, developed boils and kept falling, although she had her wheelchair with her. Mrs Coetzee was in such a state when she brought her back to hostel at the beginning of term.

Abstract from Assessment Report by St. Giles Rehabilitation Centre – February 1985

Early academic years

Academic progress in my late primary school years had slowed down and it was decided that I should be held back a year in grade 6 in order to give me a better chance. The experience of staying behind while my friends went on to the next grade was a bitter one and I felt belittled.

However, life goes on and I soon made peace with the fact that I was a year behind.

In the mid-eighties, the schooling section of the Rehabilitation Centre was expanded and my grade was privileged enough to be the first group to have our class in the new section of the school. We felt very important!

As in the past, we had some excellent teachers. At one stage, a professional artist began visiting our class once a week for about two months. We were under the impression that she had just come to simply give art classes, having no idea that she was on the scout for artwork, done by a disabled person, that was good enough to be printed. In one of these art classes, I tried to paint a picture of Father Christmas. Trying to control the strokes of the paintbrush took every ounce of concentration I possessed, but for some reason, I was so determined to pour my very best into this picture. The artist took note of my effort. A few weeks after, she stopped coming to give us classes. I was told, much to my disbelief, that my picture had been chosen to be printed on Christmas cards as part of a disability awareness campaign. I was truly overwhelmed and my family was so very proud of me.

A once in a lifetime opportunity

In 1986, a group of six children and three members of staff from St Giles were chosen to go overseas to the United Kingdom. The trip was fully sponsored by a big organisation (Stoke Mandeville Hospital is a large National Health Service hospital in Aylesbury, England). I was one of six children who were chosen from St Giles to go on this three-week trip. The disabilities of the other five children ranged from hearing impairment, paraplegia and Cerebral Palsy of a far more severe degree than mine. Four of the other children came from poor families. Even at the age of twelve, I had a very good understanding of just how privileged I was. The only money my parents needed to contribute was for my pocket money; the rest had been taken care of.

The build-up to our departure date was incredible. Though much preparation was involved, the excitement just grew as passport photos were taken and as each travel document or letter of permission was completed and signed.

The evening we were due to board the plane finally came. As my mother said goodbye, she jokingly commented that I should not come back looking like a "punk-rocker". The ten hour flight was long and I realised even then that there are so many other people in this world who are much less fortunate than me! Two of the children in our group were unable to walk at all. Special medical arrangements had to be made for them as a result of not being able to get to the toilet during the flight. I know that they experienced a great deal of discomfort and I was so very thankful for the fact that I could at least walk to the toilet on the plane.

My mother had made contact with one of the ladies in the United Kingdom who was in charge of organising the trip. As a result, this lady made it possible for us to visit Cornwall, to a little town completely off route, for a couple of days. I had never met my great-grandmother, or my grandmother's sister and brother, all of whom lived in Cornwall and it was on this trip that I became the first and only cousin to meet these precious family members. While the rest of the group stayed in Cornwall and did their own thing, I stayed with my family, who spoilt me rotten. They really gave me the time of my life and it was an extremely tearful occasion when we had to say our goodbyes.

Being only twelve years old, unfortunately, I remember only snippets of the trip, but the things I do remember are cherished memories.

As we prepared for our journey home, I noticed that one of the helpers involved with our group was in possession of an illuminated, multi-coloured "punk-rockers" wig. The wicked streak in me illuminated itself and I borrowed the wig, agreeing to mail it back upon our return. Our plane made its landing in Zimbabwe and one of my teachers helped me put the wig on. As I was carried down the stairs of the plane, I looked up onto the balcony to see my mum eagerly waving and waiting to see her daughter. Upon realising that the girl with the luminous hair being carried out of the plane was her daughter, her delightful wave turned into an angry raging fist. It was clear that Mum did not approve of my new hairstyle. As I looked down towards the bottom of the stairs, I saw the Zimbabwean television news crew waiting for us. A group of disabled children returning from a trip to the United Kingdom was big news, but an added bonus was that one of them had turned into a "punk-rocker"! Needless to say, most of the television footage was of the disabled kid who had returned home with luminous hair and our once-in-a-lifetime trip ended with much laughter.

Life in the African bush

Just after the trip to the United Kingdom, my parents moved up to the north of Zimbabwe to an area not far from Kariba. Kariba at that time was a little town on a hill, surrounded by wild African bush. Dad had been offered a job on a banana farm and although it meant that school would be a four-hour drive away from home, the fact that we would be living in the wild was very exciting. Each room of our house led off one long veranda, thus every room overlooked the great Lake Kariba. In the front garden was a beautiful swimming pool, situated under what was said to be one of the only two coconut trees in Zimbabwe. Walking out of our front gate, one would step onto the jetty, where we sat on many an evening watching beautiful sunsets over the lake with the magnificent call of the Fish Eagle in the background. Now and then, we would see the eyes of crocodiles bobbing above the water and a noise that became very familiar to us was the laughter of the hippopotami in the water just below the house. At night, the lake was speckled with the lights from hundreds of kapenta boats. Kapenta are fresh water sardines and are a delicacy in African culture. This fish is caught at night using kapenta rigs. These rigs use mercury lights connected to portable generators to attract the fish to the rig. A dip net, measuring roughly six metres in width and around eight to ten metres in length, is then used to bring the fish up from anything from 40 metres below the water.

In the still of the night, one would often hear the deep grunting of lions in the distance.

Almost every Sunday, we would go out onto the lake with the boat and cooler boxes full of refreshments and baskets full of food and we would spend the whole day fishing, returning with nets full of fish (most of the time) and with sunburnt bodies.

Very often, on these occasions, I would try my own hand at fishing, but Dad would have to help with putting the worm on the hook, casting, reeling in and very often, untangling my line. Of course, this took up much of his own fishing time, but he knew that it wouldn't be long before I got bored with sitting, dangling my rod over the boat, hoping for a bite and would occupy myself with other things. On one occasion, Dad prepared my hook, cast my rod, waited a while and then handed me my rod. I sat watching and waiting in anticipation for a bite, ready to experience the thrill of striking and trying to reel in that huge fish. After a good ten minutes, my parents could not contain themselves any longer and burst out laughing telling me to reel my line in. Upon doing so, much to my surprise, I found that dangling at the end of my line was a small fish! Oblivious to me, it had been there ever since my dad had handed me my rod. Fishing was clearly not one of my talents!

Seeing the road blocked by lions enjoying an afternoon nap, or driving cautiously past a herd of elephant, was not uncommon whenever we made our trips into Kariba to do our shopping. Mum was privileged enough to see a pack of wild dogs on one of her trips.

Living in Kariba was a privilege only a few get to experience.

On one of our many camping trips, we visited a place called Mana Pools. Being on the banks of the Zambezi River, it was a beautiful camping resort and very wild. Within the span of only two days, we had counted seventy-two elephant sightings. We went in a ten-ton truck, the back of which was fairly exposed, apart from being surrounded by thick mesh. We parked the truck under a *Kigelia pinnata* tree, better known as the sausage tree, not realising that the fruit of this tree is an attraction to the elephant. There was a full moon and as the four of us lay in the back of the truck on our stretchers, we could watch and enjoy all the nightlife by moonlight. It was all a thrill until an old elephant bull light-footedly appeared from out of the bush and headed straight for the sausage tree, the one under which we were parked. It was truly an awesome experience having this huge beast towering over us, even being able to hear the rumbling of his stomach, knowing that he could effortlessly overturn that truck in a blink of an eye. We tried to lie as still as possible, not wanting to provoke him in any way. To complicate matters, I had a persistent cough and was quietly but firmly told to cough into my pillow. The old bull eventually silently disappeared back into the bush and we were able to relax and fall asleep.

This is but one of the many amazing, unforgettable encounters in the African bush that we, as a family, were privileged to experience.

Wheeling and squealing

In the middle of 1987, we went down to South Africa, towing our caravan on a family holiday. We went down to the South coast of KwaZulu Natal. I was thirteen and Cristo almost nine years old.

We stayed in a caravan park not far from the beach. Unfortunately, bad weather prevented us from going down to the beach, as it was windy and drizzly for days on end. Cristo and I were bored and restless from having to spend most of our time in the caravan, except for the odd trip to the shops. On the occasion when the rain let up, but it was still overcast, Cristo would take me for long walks, pushing me along in my wheelchair around the caravan park. Mum had told us not to go on these walks, as it was not acceptable to have an eight-year-old pushing his older sister around in the wheelchair. However, Cristo and I did not pay any attention to her request and continued our expeditions in the park. The more we rode around, up and down steep hills and over speed humps, the more confident Cristo became with his driving skills. There was a particularly steep hill that had a speed hump at the bottom of it.

On one occasion, we made our way up to the top of the hill, turned the chair around, then Cristo climbed onto the back of the chair and away we went speeding down the hill, squealing with excitement as we sped downwards. It was not long before our squeals turned into horrified shrieks as the wheelchair hit the speed hump at the bottom. The wheelchair and I landed up on opposite sides of the road. An old man from a nearby camping site came over, picked both of us up and carried us back to our caravan. Mum very politely thanked the kind man and after he left, both of us were disciplined for our disobedience. About twenty minutes later, Mum couldn't understand why I was still crying: the problem was a sharp pain in my wrist! X-rays showed that I had broken my wrist and an entire day was spent in town being sent from pillar to post, the whole family going from one hospital to another, trying to find a doctor who was willing to set my wrist in a cast. The rest of our holiday turned out to be rather strained as, apart from having limited access to the sea due to my cast, holiday expenses had to be significantly cut due to the medical expenses involved with having my wrist attended to.

Secondary school in Zimbabwe

I was now thirteen and was nearing the completion of grade 7. St Giles did not offer secondary education and there was only one other school in Zimbabwe for the disabled which did offer secondary education, and that was in Bulawayo at the opposite end of the country from where we lived.

A few days after our trip to Mana Pools, my parents took me on the nine-hour drive down to Bulawayo to visit this school. My heart was heavy; I was now 13 years old and had been at St Giles from the age of 18 months. St Giles was all I had known, the place where I had grown up and where everyone knew me. Now I would be moving even further away from home, to the other side of the country! Having become accustomed to going home every second weekend since our move to Kariba, I would now only see Mum and Dad every three months, for the quarterly school holidays. One consolation for me was that an amazing couple, Bill and Irene, whom we had met on the recent holiday in South Africa, had taken me under their wings. They stayed on a plot on the outskirts of Bulawayo and they stepped in as my surrogate parents.

Yet, as we made our journey back after visiting the school, I was so very down. I was going to be dropped off at St Giles in Harare and my parents would carry on with their journey home to Kariba. I didn't want to be dropped off and couldn't understand why I couldn't just go home to be with my parents, especially as the remainder of the term was so short. It was mid-afternoon when my parents said goodbye to me. Everyone else was down at the community centre, which was the usual afternoon routine. I didn't have anyone to push me down to the centre in my wheelchair, so I decided to have a bath. The baths in the hostel were specially adapted for disabled children, so it was not a problem for me to get in and out of the bath on my own. As I sat in the bath, I began to sob. I knew that I was very different from other people. I didn't know what the future held for me and the thought of being so far from everything that I knew and loved, and leaving the only place where I felt at home, was so very overwhelming. I decided that the only escape from these heart-wrenching thoughts was to try and drown myself in the bath. That way, all our problems would be solved, I reasoned! Though very determined to do the deed, each time I dunked my head under the water, much to my utter frustration, after a few seconds my head would automatically come up out of the water and I would suck in huge life-giving breaths of air. Eventually, I gave up trying.

The end of 1987 rolled around all too quickly and my last day at St Giles was an extremely emotional one as I went around the whole rehabilitation centre, visiting each department and saying goodbyes to my teachers and to all the people who had become such a part of my life. These people had poured countless hours of physical, speech and occupational therapy into my life over the many years that I had been at the centre. Dr Dent had treated me medically for ailments ranging from light bouts of flu to severe convulsions. She had watched me growing up and she knew me almost as well as she knew the back of her hand. I hated that day.

I started at my new school the next January. Some consolation for me was that my two best friends from St Giles were also attending the new school. However, I found it extremely difficult to adapt. Out of all the children in the hostel, I was the only child from a different culture. The other children made it very clear that they had no intention of making any effort to try and accept me. As a result of very malicious actions towards me, two girls were expelled from the school. Of course, this made me even less popular with some of the other children.

I found it very difficult to eat the food which came out of the hostel kitchen. Boiled cabbage or spinach mixed with peanut butter or stiff mealie meal porridge served in sour milk were some of the dishes to which I was not at all accustomed, including the traditional mid-afternoon beverage of Mageu. Mageu is a traditional non-alcoholic drink popular among African people. It is made from fermented maize porridge and was not at all appealing to me.

Soup was on the menu for Sunday evenings and on the one occasion that I did venture to take a few mouthfuls of it, the entire hostel got food poisoning from it. The effects of food poisoning on a whole bunch of disabled people who find it difficult to get to the bathrooms speedily under normal circumstances were disastrous and unforgettable under these conditions!! So, eating was not a regular habit and I lost a lot of weight.

At this school, I also found it very difficult to keep up with my school work. I was in Form One and the volume of work had increased. There were no spare typewriters and so everything had to be handwritten. This was very tiring for me and I often wondered if my teachers were actually able to read what I had written.

Because of the distance between the school and home, I would very often fly back to Bulawayo after a vacation home. On one of my flights, I had the privilege of receiving first-class treatment. Two flight attendants had been complaining because they had to carry me up the stairs into the aircraft. Due to the fact that Annie had taught me the Shona language so well, I had understood every word they had said and politely thanked them in their own language as they buckled me into my seat. Upon realising that I had understood what they had said, I was treated like royalty for the whole duration of the flight.

Bill, Irene and their family were marvellous! They very lovingly and faithfully ensured that I spent every second weekend with them, sometimes more often. Very quickly, I became part of the family and there was a very close bond among us.

One Monday morning, as Bill dropped me off after a weekend visit, I burst into tears and clung to him, not wanting him to leave. He was then to learn that the man in charge of looking after the boys in the hostel had become too familiar with some of the girls and that the week before, he had taken the liberty of walking into the bathroom just as I was getting ready for my bath. He had apparently come to "reprimand" me for being late for a certain activity. But knowing his reputation, I was very afraid that he might have had other intentions. Upon arriving at work, Bill phoned my parents and informed them of what was going on. Within the next couple of days, my parents had collected me and taken me out of the school. I had only been in the school for nine months, but those nine months would have a lasting impact on my life. I spent the next five months at home with my parents.

Five whole months in Kariba sounds like a dream holiday, and, to a certain extent, it was. However, at the time, as a child, I did not appreciate it as much as I should have. Even so, it was good not experiencing the horrible gut feeling that I felt every time I boarded the plane back to Bulawayo before the beginning of a school term.

More thrilling bush experiences

By this time, Dad had left the banana farm and my parents were renting a house from friends at a camping resort, still on Lake Kariba. The house was small, cosy, and served to suit all our needs. Nevertheless, sharing one bathroom between my dad and I has, and always will be, an issue of desperation between us. Here, Mum and Dad made a living from catching and selling fish. We would often go out on the boat together as a family for whole days at a time, coming in at the end of the day with lovely tans and more often than not, nets full of fish. It was during this time that I, at last, proudly caught my first decent-sized bream. This time, I did it without Dad's help.

One day, during an off-peak season, the manager of the camping resort kindly allowed Cristo and me to spend a night in one of the bungalows. What an exciting adventure: our first night alone, away from home, even though the bungalow was only about twenty feet from our home. However, as darkness began to creep in, so did the fear. After all, we were in the African bush and *could an electric fence really keep predators at bay*? As children, these were real concerns. Needless to say, by six that evening, Cristo had cooked our meat on the coals outside, we had eaten and were safely locked up in our bungalow. Despite the initial fear, once inside, we really enjoyed the thrill of spending a night out in our own chalet playing card games. It seems, though, that we may not have been the only ones experiencing a bit of uncertainty about the adventure. Very early the next morning, Mum was knocking on the door with two cups of hot tea in her hands. It was obvious that, although very welcome, the tea was just an excuse to come and see if her two children were okay.

As I look back, I feel extremely blessed. I was still under the protection of my parents, but I was only in my early teens and I had already experienced so much in life, more than most able-bodied people.

"LORD, our Lord, how majestic is your name in all the earth!"

— Psalm 8:1

Chapter Three:
Survival of the Weakest

"What then shall we say to these things? If God is for us, who is against us?"

— **Romans 8:31**

It has been said that when the African Fish Eagle eggs begin to hatch, they don't all hatch at once. Incubation lasts about 44 days. This species typically rears two to three chicks every season, but lays from one to three eggs. This means that the chicks will be of different ages and different sizes. The second chick that hatches, which is smaller than its older sibling, can't compete for food, and it often dies.

Young children are very accepting of each other regardless of what differences may exist among them. However, as they enter their teenage years, life becomes a whole new ball game. The peer pressure switch is flicked on and the competition for social acceptance begins. The weak sink into depression, often drowning in drink or being entangled in the snare of drugs in order to ease the pain of rejection. The strong survive and often thrive on the satisfaction gained from belittling the weak, but after the thrill of everything wears off, they too often end up going down the same path as the weak. At this point, one would ask, *"Is there any hope for our young people?"* By the grace of God, I can answer *"yes"* and again "Yes! There is hope."

Mum tried her hand at home-schooling us and very soon gave up after her daughter, when she was asked to name five artists, proudly wrote down the names of her favourite five pop singers. Mum was horrified that I had not realised that she wanted names of famous painters but I was a typical teenager and when the word "artist" was mentioned, naturally, favourite pop artists were first to come to mind.

School in South Africa

My parents decided that it would be in the best interests of both their children if we went to schools in South Africa. The adjustment was a huge one for all of us. Cristo went to school in Messina on the Zimbabwe-South Africa border, where our cousins (also from Zimbabwe) attended school.

After dropping Cristo off, we travelled all the way through to Pretoria, the capital, nearly five hundred kilometres further south. We had, on a previous occasion, visited a number of schools for Cerebral Palsy children in Pretoria and Johannesburg and we decided on a special school in Pretoria that would best suit my needs. As my parents said goodbye to me at my new school, I was extremely emotional, not making it any easier for them, as they left to go back to Zimbabwe. I was in a strange country, and I was familiar with only a couple of words of Afrikaans, the predominant language of this city at the time.

I was held back one year and had to repeat Grade 8 because I had not completed my previous year in Zimbabwe and also because I was an immigrant to South Africa. All the personnel at the school were excellent and were prepared to walk the extra mile with anyone who was willing to try. As a result, I received many hours of extra Afrikaans lessons as well as a good number of hours of speech, occupational and physical therapy.

Just fresh out of Zimbabwe, a highlight of my occupational therapy sessions was learning how to use a computer. That just didn't happen in Zimbabwe! Imagine the absolute joy mixed with a bit of uncertainty when one day, the therapist told me that the school had approached a company in

Pretoria, who had agreed to donate a computer for me. This would enable me to cope better with my school work, as I would not have to physically write everything out, which was always a very laborious exercise for me, as well as for the poor teachers who had to read and mark my work.

I found the hostel environment so different from what I had been accustomed to. I couldn't understand why the other children complained so much about the food. We were given three meals a day and, compared to the hostel food that I had been exposed to in Bulawayo, and in my estimation, the food we were given here was fit for a king! Out of all the amazing personnel of the school, one lady especially stood out. She was the girls' hostel auntie and my family and I affectionately called her Tannie (auntie) Sunny. Tannie Sunny took me under her loving wing from the time my parents and I had said that first horrible goodbye, to the time I finally matriculated five years later. She did everything that I was physically unable to do at the time, from helping me in and out of the bath, helping me get dressed, helping me to change my bedding, to packing my clean washing away for me. She was a great pillar of strength to me, especially during the first difficult months at the school. Though later, as the dust settled and I developed my own circle of friends, I often gave her a rough time, especially when she felt that I was mingling with bad company.

Despite only starting at the school late in March 1989, I tried my utmost to catch up, even with subjects that were totally foreign to me. Much to everyone's surprise, I excelled in the June mid-year exams.

Coming from the tropical climate of Zimbabwe, I was not fully prepared for my first winter in South Africa. In Kariba, we could still swim in winter and most of the clothes I had brought with me were summer dresses, and the warm clothes that I did have were not enough. I had no idea of how cold it could get, but that first year I felt it. One day, Mrs Swanepoel, the head of the hostel, informed me that she was taking me into town that afternoon; I had no idea why. Mrs Swanepoel, accompanied by Tannie Sunny, took me into Woolworths and bought me a complete winter wardrobe on the school account. They bought at least three tracksuits, four jerseys, spencers (long-sleeved vests), socks and much more; In fact, what they bought was enough to last me the five years that I attended the school! I was overwhelmed by this gesture and motivated to try even harder at my school work.

By this time, my parents had immigrated to South Africa and had settled down in Tzaneen on a farm in the northern region. Tzaneen is a four-hour drive from Pretoria. Its climate is also tropical and coming from Kariba, it suited my parents very well. Dad worked on Dindinnie Farm which was one of the biggest mango exporters in South Africa at the time. I travelled by bus to and from Pretoria every school holiday, the bus trip being about a five-hour journey. I had the privilege of meeting some very interesting people, but sadly, I also got to experience first-hand that not everyone in this world is kind and compassionate. This world also contains some evil, selfish people.

One dark bus trip

On one of my trips home for the school holidays, I found myself sitting next to a lovely lady with whom I had enjoyed speaking. The lady got off the bus at one of the stops along the way. As the bus started up again to complete the last leg of its journey, I found that the seat next to me had remained unoccupied and I anticipated a quite peaceful end to my trip. Earlier during the journey, I had noticed an elderly man, his wife and his sister-in-law seated at the back of the bus. I especially noticed them as every time the bus came to a halt, they would all get off and have a cigarette. A little while into the last leg of our journey, I was surprised to find that the elderly man had made his way to the front and was occupying the empty seat next to me. I found this a little strange but didn't think too much of it and soon, I was taking part in conversation with the man. It was evening and the sun was setting; fear followed as the darkness enveloped us. The man had placed his hand on my leg and it was very clear that he had other intentions. I became very silent, not sure what to do. My main focus was to try and push his hand away and keep him from acting out his intentions.

Much to my relief, the journey soon came to an end. Mum found it very odd that I was first in line to get off, unlike usual when I always waited for everyone else to get off the bus before I made my slow exit. She was furious when, on the way home, I told her what had happened. As a result of this experience, I realised there are many wolves in sheep's clothing on this earth.

Rejection by the "strong"

The school also catered for children with remedial problems and there were far more children with remedial problems compared to those with physical disabilities. In fact, among the children my age, I was the most severely physically handicapped person.

Despite my good academic progress, I was finding the social adjustment very difficult. I was in a new country; I didn't know anybody in Pretoria and the only word of Afrikaans I knew well was "dankie" (thank you). The other children were very hostile towards me. Because I was so different from them, they were under the impression that they would be expected to do everything for me. The idea was not very appealing to them and they made sure that I knew how they felt. It was a very hard time for me. Not only was I trying to adjust to my new life in South Africa, but I was a teenager, and the realities of my limitations were setting in, often leaving me feeling like I'd been kicked in the stomach, and feeling very angry with God. *"Why had He made me so different? Why couldn't my peers accept me? Would I be accepted by anyone, not to mention have a boyfriend like all the other girls?"*

My peers knew that I couldn't understand Afrikaans and would often talk about me in my presence. I would know that they were talking about me by their body language and it hurt really badly. The fact that I had a good relationship with all my teachers and other school personnel only added fuel to the fire. At times, they entertained themselves by pouring jugs of water into my bed at night and watching while I struggled to change the sheets. When the thrill of that wore thin, they resorted to putting a drawing pin in my bed, just where I would sit. Knowing how hard I flopped down onto my bed, they enjoyed watching as I struggled to get up as fast as I'd gone down. When the thrill of only one drawing pin had worn thin, they resorted to scattering drawing pins all over the bed, sticking through from under the bottom sheet. So, each time I rolled over, another drawing pin would make its presence painfully felt.

The social rejection that I was experiencing only motivated me to try even harder at my school work. I realised, as a young teenager, that I was very different physically from everyone else and so, if I wanted to get anywhere in life, I needed to make up for my physical limitations by excelling intellectually. I didn't want to be better than anyone; I just wanted a fair chance. I knew that I would have to work hard for that chance.

A crack in the door

I was given the nickname "Spaz" (short for spastic). Instead of getting all upset about it, I laughed with the children and even referred to myself as "Spaz", making jokes about my spastic condition. At first, the children were dumbfounded. That was not the reaction they had been hoping for. As time went on, they realised that they could not help but laugh with me and friendships began to develop. I realised that making jokes about my disability was a very effective tool, useful to teach others that I am not mentally handicapped and also to help put people around me at ease about my disability. Ever since then, I have used this tool to build relationships with the people around me.

Unfortunately though, as with almost everything, too much of a good thing becomes a bad thing. Having learnt that I did in fact have the ability to make my peers laugh, thus causing them to become more accepting of me, I began to misuse my newfound tool. In order to gain better acceptance among more children, I began using extremely coarse language, making sure, of course, that none of the staff were around when I used it. You see, I was a people-pleaser, doing almost anything to please the people around me. I cared about being accepted by all, all except the most important of all; God. I was very far from God. I knew it, but didn't care much to do anything about it. To my peers, it was very funny to see a spastic person using such bad language, and even funnier when I started telling jokes of the most vulgar nature.

Imagine the attention I enjoyed when in an isolated area of the school, on a few occasions, I took a puff of my friend's cigarette? Thankfully, smoking did not appeal to me and I never made a habit of it.

Unique tests and exams

For tests or exams, I had to sit in a storeroom with my teachers and dictate answers to questionnaires. This procedure is called "Amanuensis" and was essential because writing was so difficult and writing with speed was impossible. 5% was always deducted from my mark because, for some reason, it was perceived that you were at more of an advantage if you dictated your answers to the teacher. If anything, having a teacher sitting next to you during a test or exam makes one even more nervous. I felt that the 5% deduction from my mark was unfair because no matter how I tried, I would never be able to get a 100% mark.

Late in my first year at the school, I was presented with my computer. The school acquired a special trolley on which the computer was pushed from class to class. A special little nook in the girl's hostel passage was assigned as my little study, where I studied and did my homework. The computer opened up a whole new world for me. What a pleasure it was for me to be able to type a whole essay without becoming exhausted from writing. Thankfully, I was able to start typing the answers to my tests and exams and a few times, at last, I was able to hit that 100% mark. However, for mathematics I still needed to dictate my answers to the teacher.

It was during the year-end exams that I experienced a very valuable lesson regarding the computer. Though the importance of "saving" had been drummed into me, some lessons in life are better learnt by experience. I had just about completed a whole English written exam, full of letters and stories, when one of the other students accidentally pulled the wrong plug out of the wall. The wrong plug happened to be the plug to my computer. I had not saved and I lost everything! Although the teacher very graciously gave me more time to rewrite the exam, I was tired and didn't do as well as I would have normally done. This lesson was one not easily forgotten.

The door flung wide open

Acquiring the computer also resulted in the door to social acceptance being swung wide open. I had a computer and on the computer were computer games, which most children love. In those early years of computers, computer games were not as common and easily available to children as they are today. Now I was one up on my peers and had more friends than I had ever dreamt of having.

At the end of Grade 8, my first year, my parents very proudly watched their daughter being presented with two trophies and a pack of certificates at the year-end prize-giving ceremony.

About nine months after my arrival at the school, I developed long eyelashes on a boy two years older than myself. Sean and his family had also come from Zimbabwe quite a few years earlier and Sean had grown up in South Africa. Every time Sean would enter the room, I felt the butterflies in my stomach, even though I knew that the chances of him feeling the same for me were very slim, if at all. Sean did not have a physical disability. One evening, Sean wrote a little message of about five words to me in my school diary. Although the content of the message had no implication alluding towards a deeper relationship other than friendship whatsoever, I read and reread that message over a hundred times. I wouldn't even throw the diary away at the beginning of the next school year, not wanting to lose that message! A good friendship developed between Sean and me and though I thought the world of him, I never dreamed that he would feel the same. Apparently, he did. In fact, he was facing quite a personal dilemma. Sean was a grade higher than I was and his classmates were all physically normal and a bunch of big shots, living rough lives. He was often looked down upon by them and also longed for their acceptance. *"What would they think if he started dating Spaz?"* However, not all of Sean's class was made up of rebels. There were about three other decent boys in that class and two of them were in the hostel. Not long after I turned sixteen, much to my surprise, Sean asked me out. I was later to find out that Dale, one of his two classmates, who were in the hostel, had challenged him to go against the flow and act on his feelings.

At first, it was hard for Sean, as he really received much ridiculing from his peers. At one stage, he almost broke it off but decided to hang in and endure. It was not long before Sean's peers gave him a break and accepted our relationship, though I never tried to mingle with them.

Our relationship was a very unique and special one. We really loved each other very deeply. Though we would see each other every day, except over weekends, when Sean went home to his family, we would write or type letters to each other every day, and discreetly leave them at each other's places in the hostel dining room. Those letters meant the world to me and I kept them pasted in a scrapbook for a good 14 years. One morning, on my way to school, pushing my school bag in the wheelchair, I had a fall, scraping my hands and knees on the tarmac. Sean was already at school, chatting with his big shot classmates but, upon hearing of my fall, he was in the sickbay in a flash, dictating to the nursing sister on how to clean and dress my wounds. The sister became so irritated with him that she ended up chasing him out of the sickbay. One day, two months into our relationship, Sean very solemnly sat me down and said that he had something very upsetting but confidential to tell me. Then he dropped the bombshell:

He and his family would be emigrating to Australia in two months' time. I was shattered. I would never see him again. And because the news was confidential, I could not even share my grief with my best friend. During those last two months, Sean and I spent much time together. Of course, this resulted in my school marks not being as good as usual, and as a result, I had Mrs Swanepoel breathing down my neck. I was devastated at the thought of Sean leaving, but there was nothing I could do about it. Sean's final week at school had arrived all too quickly and by this time everyone knew that he was leaving. Dale, being the good friend that he was, got permission to use the hostel kitchen that Monday evening after all the staff had gone home. He and his best friend Brett laid out a lovely dinner, which included a beautiful candle-lit table, a juicy roast beef and vegetables as well as a   delicious dessert.   The farewell was enjoyed by Andrea (a mutual friend), Dale, Brett and the two guests of honour, Sean and myself. Upon our entrance, Dale pinned a corsage on both of us and made it an evening to remember.

The trauma of Sean's emigration resulted in me suffering a mild convulsion just a few days before his departure. Thankfully, that was the last convulsion I ever experienced.

Sean and I corresponded with each other for four years after he had left. I always eagerly waited for his letters.   In 1993, I got a letter from Sean, stating his intention to come back, marry me and take me back to Australia with him. That was the last time I ever heard from him. Perhaps realising the implications of what he had said shocked him into everlasting silence.

Real acceptance

About a year after Sean had left, I attended a function which was an outreach project held by a Wesleyan Church, not far from the school. There I met many wonderful people. After expressing my desire to attend the church regularly, Pastor Stanley graciously organised transport for me with various members of his congregation so that I could start attending church every Sunday. I thoroughly enjoyed the services and built up some very good relationships, specifically with the Bams. The Bam family was a precious one. There was Violet, her husband Chris and their three children; Brett, Sherryne and Darrell. Chris and Violet were very receptive people, always welcoming young people into their home.

Brett and Sherryne both participated in ballroom dancing and took part in many competitions. Violet often organised front-row competition tickets for me and I would go and spend whole Saturdays watching all participants from toddlers right up to the professionals. What a treat, though I often felt drawn to the dance floor to join them. I was certain that if I did not have cerebral palsy, I would have been a dancer.   Brett went on to become a South African champion.

It was during this time that I responded to a Gospel message, preached by our pastor one Sunday morning. The Lord opened my eyes to the fact that I am a sinner in desperate need of a Saviour. I had heard during the service that Jesus had paid the price for my sins by dying on a cross two thousand years ago. The Lord showed me that Sunday that He is the only who could redeem me. Through His blood alone could I enjoy a relationship with God the Father, obtain eternal life and even live a meaningful life here on earth, despite my limitations. That day, Jesus became Lord of my life as I confessed with my mouth that Jesus is Lord and believed in my heart that He had died for me on the cross - Romans 10:9.

The joy I experienced was unspeakable. I went back to the hostel bubbling and for the next few days, nobody could keep me quiet.

My "friends" became weary of me. They had no idea what I was on about. Over time, I stopped swearing and telling dirty jokes and lost my so-called friends.   I was no longer "Spaz" but instead, I became "Holy Joe". Something about me made them uncomfortable and they didn't like it. Instead of becoming depressed about it, I held on to Romans 8:31 which says *"...If God is for us, who is against us?"*

Each evening, after much prayer, I would take my Bible into the dining room and lounge where everyone was watching television. I would call one person aside and give him or her the gospel message. Within two weeks, eleven people professed to have come to Salvation. I got permission to use a classroom on Thursday evenings, where I conducted a Bible study. As I look back now, I often wonder if that was a very wise thing to do, as my own knowledge of God and His Word was so limited. But in reality, it is God who speaks through His Word; He sees the motives of the heart and He can even use an ignorant seventeen-year-old to do His work and further His Kingdom!

Though I had lost most of my friends at school, I had been blessed with a good support system at church. The Bam family became my closest friends and many very special memories were born out of my association with this family. I spent almost every Saturday afternoon with them. I often wonder how they managed to put up with this weekly visit, which would persist for the next three years of their lives. I praise God for this family and their wonderful friendship and hospitality towards me. Their support really helped me to accept myself for who I really am; a child of God, fearfully and wonderfully made. God, the Creator of all things, had not only created me but had taken the time to make me different. I knew He had done this for a specific reason. This new revelation filled me with amazing joy and a peace that truly surpasses all understanding.

Living in a large dormitory with about eight other girls made it very difficult to have a daily quiet time with the Lord. Out of desperation, I started going to sit in a little back room which was cold and musty. The night helper occupied it when she was on duty and was not too concerned about the state in which it was. However, that little room served as a wonderful haven into which I could slip away and have some very special times with the Lord, reading the Word, praying and even singing hymns out loud. Nobody could hear me; it was just my Lord and me.

I joined the Friday night youth group of which Chris Bam was the leader. Over time, I gained many friends through this group of young people. We were a close group and did many things together, ranging from outreaches to orphanages to ten pin bowling and even camping. On our social outings, we would often enjoy watermelon and being the sucker that I am, nine out of ten times, I would be the one to start a melon fight. Because I could not run away, I always ended up a sitting duck being pelted by melon skins. Of course, I could not take part in many of the activities due to my limitations, but I was always included even if it was just to go along for the ride.

For my eighteenth birthday, Chris and Vi, along with the rest of the youth group, organised a surprise birthday party. I felt so very blessed by all the love that was shown by these people.

The school was supportive of my involvement with the church and often graciously provided me with transport to church or the Bams' residence. However, Mrs Swanepoel naturally gave me a curfew and monitored my outings closely.

Brett and I were especially good friends. His encouragement resulted in me trying my hand at all sorts of outrageous things, which included me diving into a swimming pool and trusting that he would be right there to retrieve me from the floor of the pool, or rowing a canoe, on my own on the Hartbeespoort Dam in Pretoria. To an extent, Brett tried to teach me certain survival skills in the water, such as how to float. He also tried to teach me how to swim without the aid of a tube, but that didn't prove to be possible.

In grade 9, I had already secretly decided that Brett would be the perfect escort for me to my matric farewell dance, three years into the future.

Faith crushed or strengthened?

As a new Christian, at times, I leaned more towards the charismatic side of Christianity. One Sunday, I attended a church service with a friend in Johannesburg. This congregation believed that a sure sign of salvation was if one possessed the gift of speaking in tongues, something I could not do. I consoled myself by the fact that perhaps due to my speech impediment, I could not exercise that gift – as if a speech impediment could hinder the Power of God. That same weekend, the church was holding a Sunday healing service. My friend insisted that we attend the service. She was so excited and felt confident that it would be there that I would be healed. Her excitement was contagious and though I had been disappointed years before, I couldn't help but start getting my hopes up again. *"Maybe previously the time had not been right. Maybe God wanted me to come to salvation first and then He would heal me so that I could parade the miracle far and wide, thus glorifying His Name."*

The service proceeded and our excitement finally reached its climax when an appeal was extended to all who needed healing to go forward. My friend and I went up and what happened next could have either crushed or strengthened my faith in Christ.

As we were standing in front, trained people from the church came and stood behind us. As the pastor prayed for each person, he or she would fall backward onto the ground, their fall broken by the person standing behind them and they would laugh hysterically. This was called being "slain in the Spirit". I wondered what would happen to me! Upon reaching me, the pastor laid his hand on my forehead; nothing happened and all of a sudden, I felt him give my forehead an extra push. Being unsteady on my feet, of course, I fell backwards and before I knew it, I was on the ground. Everyone around me was laughing hysterically, everyone except me! Not only was I not healed but I had not been "touched" as everyone else had. I wondered what was wrong with me or whether I was really a Christian. I wondered why God had passed me by.

The next Sunday after church, poor Pastor Stanley was bombarded with questions. Patiently, he walked me through Scripture, showing me that nowhere in the Bible does anyone fall backwards in hysteria, but instead, we see examples of people falling forward on their faces in reverence to God. He also showed me, from 1 Corinthians chapter 14, that speaking in tongues is not a sign of salvation; it is a gift, a gift of languages. I began to wonder if instead of passing me by, God had, in fact, blessed me by protecting me from taking part in the chaotic hysteria.

On another occasion, on a Friday night, Brett and I, along with a few others from our youth group, attended a service at another church. Well-known international performers would be performing at that church and it was advertised that healing would be part of the service. Once again, allowing my hopes to soar, I went, believing with all my heart that I would be healed. At the end of the performance, anyone seeking healing was invited into a side room where the performers would pray for them. I went into the side room accompanied by Brett.

When it was my turn to receive prayer, one of the performers laid his hand on my head and began to pray. As he was praying, I experienced the strangest sensation: it was almost like a very mild electric current was pulsating from my heart, through my head to his hand and back down to my heart. When he had finished praying and was about to move on to the next person, I looked up at Brett, and, through the flow of tears, begged him to call the performer back and make him beseech God for my physical healing, thinking that maybe he had misunderstood my prayer request. Poor Brett was placed in a rather awkward situation. Brett did as I had asked and the performer's reply to us was one that would change my life. He gently told me that perhaps it had not been God's will to heal me at that time. I appreciated the fact that he acknowledged the Sovereignty of God. Then, without me mentioning a word, he confirmed what I had felt during his prayer for me. He said that, while praying for me, he had felt the strongest spirit within me that he had ever felt. I knew that this was not a fabrication because I had felt it too. The performer said that he believed that God wanted to use me just as I am in very big ways. This time, I went home rejoicing. God had not been obligated to, but He had chosen to show me in a very tangible way, that I was His child and that the time for my healing was in His hands. And in the meantime, He would use me in ways I had never dreamed of.

This was confirmed in a conversation I had with one of my teachers not long after this incident. He agreed with me that if God had healed me, the impact of the healing would have been far-reaching, but *"how long would the impact have lasted?"* he asked. He also observed that before long, I would have slipped into everyday life, taking it for granted and forgetting what it had been like to be so dependent on God for the help of others. Finally, and most importantly of all, he commented that in my present disabled state, God could use me more and continuously in so many ways (even in ways unknown to me) every day in the lives of people around me. This conversation would also have a lasting impact on my life.

The victorious survival of the weak

Just before entering my final year, I was moved out of the large dormitory where I'd been staying, into a little double room. It had been a simple bathroom that contained a small basin and washing area. I shared the room with Brigetta, a Portuguese girl. Ironically, when Brigetta first arrived at the school, she was very wary of my Cerebral Palsy. She had never been exposed to it before and had no clue as to what it was all about or how to treat me. Now we were sharing a room. Brigetta, though very short, became very protective over me and had a very kind heart, taking it upon herself to help me wherever she could. Much laughter could often be heard coming from that little room and very soon she became my best friend.

By this time, children at the school, in my Grade as well as Grades higher than mine, had also developed a special kind of affection and sense of protection towards me. Even the rough and tough guys always had a kind word to say to me and I am certain this came about as a result of the change they had seen in me.

One Friday night, I stayed up late along with a few older children, enthralled in cracking the password which would take us onto the next level of the computer game we had been playing for months. On my way to bed, tired and very shaky on my feet, I had a fall, one that I will never forget. I lost my balance and smashed my head against the passage railing. The bang was so loud that the girls in their dormitories mistook the sound to be that of a door slamming shut until they heard the awful screams which followed. The older boys with whom I had been playing the computer games heard my screams from their passage and came running. As they lifted me up off the ground, the blood gushed from my head and people began to panic. Thankfully, upon closer examination, the wound in my head turned out to be tiny and the intense bleeding was just normal for a head wound, regardless of how small. The fact that my injuries were very minor did not stop the boys from helping the matron who was on night duty to cut away strands of my hair, clean and tend to the wound that night. What a contrast to what I had experienced from the children when I first arrived at the school a few years before!

Final days at school

Four years had flown by all too quickly and before I knew it, I was in Grade 12, my final year. This was an extremely challenging year for me. As if the heavy workload was not enough, I was suffering severely from tonsillitis. I would get it almost every month and because my immunity was so low, my mouth ulcers would intensify and this made it very difficult for me to eat. Many days were spent in bed trying to recover, but at the same time, many valuable school hours were lost. During the April school holidays, I went into hospital and had my tonsils removed. The operation, though minor for small children, was extremely painful for me, a nineteen-year-old. For two weeks thereafter, my parent's house was a very peaceful place because it was too painful for me to talk. Much to our relief, I made a quick recovery and my health greatly improved.

However, my challenges were not over. The computer, which I had received nearly four years earlier, had been very reliable, despite having been pushed around from class to class every day at school. But now it was starting to give me problems and I was due to write my finals in the October of that year, so I needed a reliable computer.   This time, the school was not in the position to assist me and I knew that I needed to make a plan quickly. After much prayer, I approached the school and asked for their permission to initiate my own fundraising project. Having obtained their permission, I typed out a standard letter, explaining who I was and my predicament, asking for any kind of donation. I then sat with the telephone directory, writing out long address lists including every company in Pretoria that I could find, from big well-known companies to small little ice cream factories and posted my letter to each of them, prayed and then waited. Two weeks later, much to my absolute joy, I received my first cheque; it was for one hundred Rand. Though I was so excited, I knew that I would need much more if I was going to get that new computer in time.   But God is so faithful; very slowly, more one-hundred-Rand cheques arrived in the post for me and a few months later, I had one thousand Rand. Imagine how important I felt when two other boys from my class went into a shopping mall with me, not far from the school, and opened my first bank account. My occupational therapist's husband was a computer expert and kindly agreed to build up a more updated computer for me for a thousand Rand; I was over the moon! I received it about six weeks before I was due to write my finals and much to my awe, this one even had a colour monitor and I am almost certain that it cost him more than one thousand Rand to build.

My fairytale evening

The Matric Farewell we had been looking forward to for so many years was approaching fast. This once-in-a-lifetime evening more than often ends up costing parents of young girls thousands of Rands as each girl competes in the world of fashion, trying to out-dress each other and out-do the standard set by girls in previous years. In my head, I had a picture of the dress I wanted. It was not one that would top the fashion charts; in fact, quite the opposite: my idea of the perfect dress came out of the sixties' era. I wanted a ballroom-style dress, one that was long and would flare out at the bottom. I had resigned myself to the fact that the chances of me getting that kind of dress were very slim and so I didn't put much effort into looking for such a dress. My parents were not among the wealthiest but they tried their best. We went from shop to shop trying on dresses that looked beautiful in shop windows but upon fitting them, they looked terrible because of my posture.

One afternoon, upon returning from a fruitless day of window shopping and dozens of fittings, feeling very despondent, my mother went to my cupboard to look for something. I was speechless. *"Did Mum really think she would find something good enough for a matric dance in my cupboard?"* Mum pulled out an old green lace dress. The dress had been given to me four years earlier by a bunch of girls who were trying to get rid of it because it was so ugly and old-fashioned. By giving it to me, they thought they were being spiteful. The dress had been too small for me at the time but nevertheless, I had kept it all those years and now, Mum was suggesting that I try it on! Finding comfort in the fact that it would be too small, I humoured Mum and tried it on. Much to Mum's joy (and my horror), the dress fit perfectly. I had to go through and show Dad. *"Surely Dad would agree that this was no dress for a matric dance,"* I thought. Instead, Dad loved it and insisted that with gold-coloured shoes and a gold-coloured belt, it would be perfect! *"Yeah right,"* I thought, *"perfect recipe for the most outrageous looking girl at the dance."* However, after seeing myself in the mirror, I decided that perhaps it didn't look that bad. In fact, I rather liked the colour as well as the length. I liked how perfectly the top half fit.

When I took it back to Pretoria, Violet also fell in love with it and organised for me to borrow a three-layered petticoat. Upon fitting it with the petticoat, much to my absolute surprise, I found that I was wearing the dress I had dreamed of wearing to my matric farewell! It was beautiful, and straight out of the sixties' era. This was just the start of an amazing outpouring of so many blessings.

I was not in the business of competing in fashion and I expected to be lost in the glamour of girls who had gone all out to compete with each other.

However, as a result of the kindness of so many people, this would prove to be the most magical evening of my life. Quite contrary to what I had originally expected! An orthopaedist in Pretoria kindly and lovingly built my gold shoes up for me, free of charge.

I had not built up the courage to ask Brett to be my partner for that evening and so he took it upon himself to ask me if I would like him to be my escort. What a privilege to have one of my closest friends, not to mention a South African champion dancer, take me to my farewell. Brett took the time to try and teach me a few simple dance moves. This resulted in many precious moments of laughter, but, in the end, I caught on to the moves in my own special way.

The big day finally arrived and all the girls in my class were treated to facials. Few people have experienced the personal, very special treatment by hairdressers the way I have. That afternoon, my hairdresser arrived with a bunch of beautiful flowers for me in one hand and a bottle of champagne to celebrate the occasion in the other. He did not charge me a cent. His mother was one of the hostel matrons and he had been doing my hair for quite some time. He had closed his salon for the afternoon especially to come and do my hair and he had even brought his assistant. While he did my hair, his assistant did my nails as well as my makeup. I had long thick hair which he put up into a French roll, decorating it with a couple of white freesias and an array of other little flowers.

Just after 17:00 pm, Brett (armed with a bunch of red carnations), Sherryne and Violet arrived to take photos. They were amazed at the magic the hairdresser and his assistant had worked on me. We couldn't help but laugh as one of the kids back at the school commented that I looked like a fairy. The venue was very elegantly decorated and everyone else looked wonderful. The cuisine was delicious and enjoyed by all. Brett and I had a very enjoyable evening and there was much laughter on the dance floor. Brett and Violet took me back to the school just before midnight, where faithful Tannie Sunny was waiting to help remove all the pins from my hair and to help me out of my dress. I was very grateful for Tannie Sunny because I know that if I had tried to undo my own hair, it would have ended up looking worse than a bird's nest.

Final exams

The fun was now over and it was time to get down to serious studying: the final exams were due to start the following month. As exam time drew nearer, I isolated myself more and more, very grateful for the privacy of our little room. Deep into the exams, however, the four walls of the room started getting to me. I was becoming tired from the constant day and late-night studying, but I refused to go out and enjoy a bit of social time with the others. Eventually, Tannie Sunny, seeing what a state I was getting myself into, came into the room one day and insisted that I go out with her for a walk. I wondered if she was crazy as I was sitting a huge exam the next day and I needed every moment I had to study. But Tannie Sunny would not take "no" for an answer and so I went out with her. I was so thankful that I did because getting out into the fresh air did me the world of good. It seemed to help clear my mind, and, upon returning to my books, I was able to concentrate much better.

Though very stressful, the exams went better than expected and before we knew it, they were over and it was time to say our goodbyes. Once again, I found this very difficult. I had started at the school, new to South Africa, scared and lonely - but had fought my way up the academic ladder and through very muddy waters to social acceptance, beating all the odds of survival. Most importantly, I had come to know the Lord as my personal Saviour. The scales had fallen from my eyes and I had begun to see how very intimately involved the Lord really is in our lives. I had seen His amazing provision and how He had taken care of situations where there seemed to be no hope. I knew that this was but a taste of what was to come. With my whole life ahead of me, the anticipation of what the future held was so exciting. Though weak, I knew He had a plan for me; I knew it wouldn't be easy, but I also knew that He would carry me on His Almighty wings through it all.

> *"He gives strength to the weary, And to him who lacks might He increases power. Though youths grow weary and tired, And vigorous young men stumble badly, Yet those who wait for the LORD will gain new strength; They will mount up with wings like eagles They will run and not get tired, They will walk and not become weary."*

— Isaiah 40:29-31

Chapter Four:
Poised for Takeoff

*O taste and see that the LORD is good; How blessed is the man
who takes refuge in Him! O fear the LORD, you His saints; For
to those who fear Him there is no want.*

— Psalm 34:8-9

The young eaglets fledge after 65-75 days. The newly airborne eagles stay close
to the nesting vicinity, still sharing food caught by their parents while
perfecting their own hunting skills.

Although very ambitious, I would soon have to come to terms with the fact
that it would still be quite a while, if ever, before I could live a fully independent
lifestyle.

College days

As the end of the year 1993 rolled into 1994, the excitement and anticipation,
mixed with a bit of uncertainty, was overwhelming. I was entering a whole new
phase in my life and I wondered what lay ahead. As a child of the most High, I
knew that whatever the future held, it could only be good. I had been accepted
into Access College, a college for physically disabled people in Johannesburg.
This was even further away from home than Pretoria was. I had signed up for
the Business Administration Course and was aiming for a diploma. I was to
start college in the middle of February, but in the meantime, I worked for my

dad's boss on the farm, sorting and selling rejected export mangoes to hawkers, waiting in anticipation for my matric results. What a celebration it was when the results finally came through and I had passed my matric with distinction.

In Johannesburg, I was booked into a little boarding house, shared by about ten other disabled people who also attended the college. The house was a good ten-minute drive away from the college. We were transported to and from college by a mini-bus.

I arrived in Johannesburg the weekend before I was due to begin college. The trip from Tzaneen to Johannesburg was long, a journey of about 450 km. The poor car was overloaded. Among other things, I really needed to take my computer which was a desktop with a monitor. These alone took up much space. Without it, there was no way that I would have been able to do my college work, which included many assignments. Unfortunately, in those days, laptops didn't exist, otherwise, it would have been so much easier. Upon arriving at the boarding house, we found that there was no table available on which to set up my computer, so my parents, not being used to the concrete jungle and busy roads of Johannesburg, bravely drove into the daunting city to purchase a table for me. As if that wasn't enough, they still had to find their way back to the boarding house with half a table sticking out the back of the trunk of the car!

That Friday afternoon after my parents had left, I watched as the mini-bus drove up the driveway and off-loaded its passengers, who were returning from a day at college. There were people in wheelchairs, other people with Cerebral Palsy, and people with amputated limbs. I really enjoyed meeting everyone, except for one person, Russell. Russell was a 27-year-old blind man. Six years earlier, he had been involved in a motorcycle accident, losing his eyesight just before qualifying as an electrician. Russell greeted me very abruptly and came across as very rude and arrogant. My mind was made up; I did not like him. A few hours after our first encounter, Russell knocked on the door of the ladies' dormitory with a handful of coins and asked me to count them for him. I thought he had quite a cheek, asking me for help after the way we had made our first acquaintance. However, as I helped him, I began to realise that perhaps he wasn't that bad after all.

I thoroughly enjoyed the college. I enjoyed meeting so many people. I enjoyed all the lectures and seminars and loved the lecturers.

Over the next few months, Russell and I developed a very good friendship. Upon completing his first course, Russell decided to stay on and take on another course. He was a very hard worker and wanted to gain as much knowledge as possible that would benefit him in his future. He wanted to enrol for the same course I was doing, which entailed bookkeeping and accounting. For Russell, this was a huge challenge. Being the first blind student at the college to take on these subjects, he found that there were no cassette tapes for the blind available on these subjects. Yet Russell was determined to beat the odds, but he needed someone to assist him. Because we stayed in the same boarding house and we had built a good friendship, I offered to assist him and walk him through the subjects of bookkeeping and accounting. He was very grateful for the offer, but at the same time, warned me that he could be very stubborn and strong-willed and that it wouldn't be an easy journey. Russell was not exaggerating: Many nights were spent burning the midnight oil. Although his computer had a voice synthesizer and he knew his way around the keyboard like a fish in water, it was my job to try and imprint the layout of each different accounting book in his mind. Before we could even start on our assignments in a specific book, Russell had to know each column's heading, how wide each column was and he would have had to have set it up on his computer using the Lotus program, dividing his columns with the colon sign. What a pleasure it would have been if Excel had been a commonly used program in those days! On test and exam days, he would be sure to come and wake me at four in the morning so that we could go over the work just one more time.

Russell and I persevered on the road of schooling, working well together, but not without the odd disagreement or moments of irritation with each other.

I may have helped him in various ways, but in many other ways, Russell assisted me. Had it not been for him helping me with Business Calculations, I would not have obtained a good result for that subject. Russell also provided a sense of security for me during my stay in Johannesburg, helping me financially on many occasions, such as providing the means for me to see a doctor once when I became chronically ill with bronchitis during winter. Russell fully understood my need for physical rest, and, using his disability to his advantage, would often burst into the ladies' dormitory in the afternoons after college while I was trying to rest before dinner, and would tell all the other ladies to please be quiet as "Debbie is resting". He knew he could get away with it since no one would protest as Russell couldn't see anything anyway!!!

At the end of it all, Russell passed his final exam with distinction.

During my time in college, I had the joy of attending the Wesleyan Church in Johannesburg, as well as Bible studies. I had built some very good relationships with various members of that congregation and especially with Pastor Winston and his dear wife Annette, with whom I am still blessed to have contact. I was very grateful for the love and support which I received from the congregation of this little church.

Daring to take the wheel

Whilst living and studying in Johannesburg, I decided to try my hand at getting my learner driver's license. I really believed that, with a few adaptations to the car, I would be able to drive! I was young and naïve. I had a mind which was as normal as any other twenty-year-old and had dreams which included living life as other twenty-year-olds around me were living life. *Yes, I was "slightly" different but it was not too serious; nothing that a bit of extra hard work could not overcome, right?* However, I didn't mention a word of it to my parents. Deep down inside, I knew that they knew better and would end up talking me out of the crazy pursuit that I was on. The director of the Association for Persons with Disabilities (APD) at the time fully supported me in my quest and helped me to obtain the study manual. He was even brave enough to let me drive his little Mazda 323 around the grounds of the boarding house. He was rather impressed with my driving skills, even though I was only driving in first gear!!

Finally, the day came for me to go for my learner's license. I took a day off from college, and, for "moral support", Russell bunked college that same day. I spent the whole morning going over what I had learnt with Russell, and at one o'clock, the wife of the APD director kindly picked me up and took me to the Traffic Department, where I was to write my exam. As I entered the examination room after paying the exam fee, an awful silence fell over the room and I could almost hear the thoughts of the other people who were taking the exam. "*What in the world does this woman think she is doing?*" Upon receiving my exam paper, I was relieved to find that not much writing was required. Most of the questions were multiple choice. Whether an applicant had passed or failed was obvious because if the applicant passed, he was then ushered to the right to take his eye test. If the applicant failed, he had to exit the examination room on the left.

I was one of the first people to complete the exam and as I got up to hand in my paper, I could feel every eye in the room on me, to see whether I would pass or fail. Imagine the utter shock wave that swept over the room as I was ushered on to the right to have my eye test!

I was overcome by such a feeling of victory as I went back to the boarding house and Russell and I celebrated that evening with a Coke and a pizza.

Only after I had completed my course in Johannesburg and had gone back home did I, in a very crafty manner, break the news of my Learner's Driver's License to my parents. One evening, we all went out to dinner and I took the learner's license along and presented it to my dear parents in the restaurant over dinner. You see, I was not sure what their reaction would be. This way, chances of overreaction were eliminated. As my parents realised what I had presented to them, they were both overcome with emotion. I was stunned: I hadn't expected tears. The tears were brought on by a mixture of pride, joy and sorrow; sorrow because they knew reality, the reality that it would be impossible for me to ever be able to drive on a public road. My muscle coordination is very poor and my muscle spasms are very profound.

The next day, however, the family humoured me as I drove my dad and my aunt around the farm in my gran's little Volkswagen. In first gear, of course!

At the end of my seven months in Johannesburg, I obtained my diploma and went home to my parents with a heart bursting with excitement and anticipation at the thought of what the future may have in store for me.

> *"Your eyes have seen my unformed substance; And in Your book were all written. The days that were ordained for me, When as yet there was not one."*

> — Psalm 139:16

Chapter Five:
Longing to Spread My Wings

"To man belong the plans of His heart, but from the Lord comes the reply of the tongue."

— **Proverbs 16:1**

Having perfected their hunting skills, the young eagles will soon have to leave the area, find a mate and establish their own territory.

As each one of us grows up, we develop an ideal in our minds as to what kind of life we would like to lead. We have dreams and goals, and, in most cases, we do everything in our power to attain our dreams and reach our goals. Very rarely, though, do we come across someone who has lived the life of his dreams, someone who has achieved all that he has set out to do without having had any obstacles to overcome. In fact, in most cases, people find themselves in places and in occupations totally different from what they'd imagined or initially set out to do.

So often we forget that each one of our lives, Christian or not, is like a jigsaw puzzle piece that fits into one magnificent picture painted by God. This picture was envisaged before the creation of the world, depicting God's absolute glory. Though we may have our own plans, it is the Lord's will for our lives that prevails. He has the final say.

"Now listen, you who say, 'Today or tomorrow we will go to this or that city, spend a year there, carry on business and make money.' Why, you do not even know what will happen tomorrow...instead you ought to say, 'If it is the Lord's will, we will live and do this or that'."

— James 4:13-15

As a young lady, fresh out of college, I still had to learn this principle.

Despair

Having obtained my diploma in Business Administration in 1994, I was filled with anticipation. I did not know what kind of future lay ahead of me, but I was excited as I held on to the knowledge that I was a child of the Most High and I clung to the fact that according to His Word, He had plans for me. I had no idea what plans He had, yet I was convinced they were good. In the eyes of the world, the chances of me finding a job and living an independent lifestyle were very slim, if not impossible.

After college, I went home and lived with my parents for 18 months on a farm 55 kilometres outside of the nearest little town of Tzaneen. This time in my life was an extremely difficult time. No longer did I enjoy the kind of church and social life that I was used to while attending school and college, and I missed it terribly. For most of that time, the only people with whom I had contact were Mum, Dad, my grandmother and the farm workers. Our pets were my constant companions during the day while everyone else was at work. I kept myself occupied by writing letters on the computer and baking. Cristo was still at boarding school in Tzaneen. He came home every weekend and I would spend time helping him with his schoolwork. I wrote many letters, applying for work in and around the little community, but all to no avail.

In time, I became very despondent; I knew there was more to life, but every time I tried to find an open door, I would walk slap bang into a rock-solid wall! The reality of my limitations would hit me like a kick in the stomach, and I would sink into depression. Though I was convinced that God was still in control, it was very hard to accept that this time in my life was indeed part of His plan for me. I could not see a future for myself, nor could I see how God could be working this all out for my good! All I could do was believe without seeing and cling to God's promises in His Word, trusting that this was all part of the plan! This time was also very hard for my family. They had no idea what would become of my life. For them, their biggest fear was what would happen to their daughter if they were to suddenly pass away. It was also very hard for them to see me so desperate. Dad would try so hard to help me make peace with, and accept, my situation. Many times, this would result in huge arguments, leaving us feeling even more desperate and, on occasion, again, thoughts of suicide became very real and very sweet in my mind.

Yet I knew that suicide was not the answer. Our main purpose in life as Christians is to glorify God in everything we do. If I had taken my life, what message would I have been sending out to the world?

It would be the message that I don't believe that God is Sovereign. That I don't believe that God uses every situation (good and bad) for His glory, and for my good. That I don't really believe that God is even interested in my life, and, in reality, I am an absolute hypocrite!

It is easy to give ourselves the Christian label but when the rubber meets the road and the time to put all trust in God comes despite all odds, to exercise true Christian living (believing without seeing), so often, we look for the easy way out. Perseverance through suffering brings glory to God and strengthens our character.

"...but we also rejoice in our sufferings, because we know that suffering produces perseverance; perseverance, character, and character, hope."

— Romans 5:3-4

Glimmers of hope

There were, however, times during this period when I was blessed with various things that kept me busy; activities that gave me a sense of worth, stimulation and hope for the future. Now and then, my dad's employer, Bill, would ask me to do computer work from home for him and for this, I was paid well! On occasion, I would visit my auntie Caroline and Uncle Henry, who lived two hours away from my parent's' home, sometimes for two weeks at a time. At the time, my aunt was not working, and so we had some wonderful times together and we were both greatly uplifted as we encouraged each other through the various trials each of us was facing.

I loved baking and cooking while I was at home. Two to three times a week, I would make dinner for the family. I loved being in the kitchen. I would sit and study a recipe. I thought the method through, trying to work out ways of doing things that were physically difficult, or even impossible, such as cracking an egg. As time passed, I managed to develop a way of cracking an egg with one hand. In the beginning, bits of eggshell would slip through my fingers and at times, Dad would lovingly joke about how "crunchy" the meal was, knowing full well that the meal was not intended to be "crunchy"! I planned my cooking in such a way so that during her last half hour of work, our house cleaner could assist me with everything which I was physically unable to do. So, when Mum returned from work, she would have to help me with the bare minimum, such as removing steaming food from the oven.

Over time, I perfected a microwave chocolate cake recipe and started my own little home industry selling chocolate cakes to people in the community.

Every Friday, I would have four to five orders for my chocolate cake. I really enjoyed running my little industry. However, I made the big mistake of manually creaming the margarine and icing sugar instead of using the electric mixer, as I had been afraid that the stiff margarine would cause the motor to burn out. As a result, it was not long before I developed tennis elbow or rather "cake arm" (as Bill called it), in my left arm. This was extremely painful! Because I could barely use my right arm for two weeks, I was totally dependent on my mum for everything, including bathing and dressing, and even feeding me. This led to even greater frustration, and all that I could see was yet another door being shut in my face! However, having realised that it was in fact possible to use an electric mixer to cream margarine, after a few weeks of rest, I was able to continue with my little baking industry.

Accepting the unacceptable

At first, my family and I would not even entertain the possibility of me living in a home or institution. It was just not the kind of place for me. I wanted to live a more fulfilled life. As the months passed and there was no improvement in my situation, we began to realise that there was no other option, and finally resigned ourselves to the fact that I would have to go into a home for the disabled. The main reason for this decision was that I would have a roof over my head and food in my stomach should something happen to my parents.

Finding the ideal place was very difficult! Many of the homes we looked at around South Africa were so impersonal. They were more like institutions, catering for really severely handicapped adults. For example, residents shared a room, including one cupboard. I so longed for my personal space. I had been in a hostel for most of my educational career, living in dormitories, and I prayed that if I had to go into a home, I would at least have my own room. Sharing a room would have meant that there would have been a limit to what I could have in my part of the room. This would mean that taking my computer with me could have posed a problem. Without my computer, I would have been like a fish out of water! Though able to write, there are very few people, apart from myself, who can actually read my writing, so the computer is such a vital part of my life! I knew that living in a home would not be easy, so I wanted a little haven into which I could go and just be myself, do what I wanted to do, play my own music, be able to read and have my quiet times in privacy.

Finally, we heard about Green Acres in Polokwane, approximately two hours from the farm. Trish Roos, the provincial social worker, invited me to a screening meeting, where I appeared before a panel so that they could decide whether I would qualify as a resident of Green Acres. During my interview, I was asked how I felt about living with intellectually impaired adults. In reply, I had said that I did not mind and that I would be willing to help the intellectually impaired in any way I could. I had not realised at the time that about 80% of Green Acres consisted of intellectually impaired adults and that it was run mainly according to their needs, regarding strict discipline and rules. After appearing before the panel, I was shown around the home. Much to my joy, I found that most of the residents had their own rooms and I came to believe that although the Green Acres was a sheltered environment, residents were able to live their lives as independently as their disabilities would allow. I began to feel that moving to Polokwane would open a whole new world of opportunities for me and I was eager to make the move. My name was placed on the waiting list and I had to wait for a room to become available. Finally, 7 months later, I received a call from Trish informing me that I would be able to move into Green Acres at the beginning of that next week, leaving us with only a couple of days to pack and get everything ready for the move.

On the 9th of April 1996, my parents helped me settle into my room. It was quite an exercise trying to comfortably fit my dressing table, bookcase, computer and more into the room. By the end of the day, though, we had managed to find a place for everything and we had made my little room very cosy.

However, my parents had not even left when the housemother came into my room and removed my little medicine case from my possession, saying that no resident was permitted to keep any form of medication in the rooms. Although I understood that keeping my medication could have been a danger to the other residents if they had gotten their hands on it, I was still humiliated by the fact that a piece of my independence was being taken away and that I would no longer be able to administer my own medication. It was then that it began to dawn on me that life in Green Acres was perhaps going to be even harder than I had originally anticipated.

Being a very shy person, I managed to get away with not going to the dining room for dinner on my first night in the home. However, on my way to the dining room for breakfast the next morning, I walked past two men in wheelchairs, about 20 years older than myself, having an argument. They were arguing about whose girlfriend the new lady in the home would be! Imagine the shock! I was soon to learn that it was the norm for a new resident to be swept off her feet even on her first day. It was not unusual for a couple to be engaged within the first month of the partner's stay in the home, nor was it unusual to be engaged more than once to different partners within a period of 2 months! Intellectually impaired people are very affectionate and keeping up to date with the circle of love in Green Acres would become very interesting.

A shining light on the hill

Having moved to Polokwane, I was eager to rebuild my church life. By the first weekend of my stay in Green Acres, I had contacted the pastor of a Church in Polokwane, introduced myself, and organised a lift to church for that Sunday. Pastor Charles and Sally had come to meet me during my first week. Although we had a good time of fellowship, I sensed a feeling of awkwardness and realised that, understandably, these people did not know much about my disability and it would take time for them to get to know me.

The church was small, comprising only 5 families, including the pastor and his wife. As always, it was not very long before everyone grew familiar with my ways and as usual, a sign of their acceptance of me was their affectionate teasing about my disability. Over a period of two years, we shared times of intimate fellowship. Apart from the usual fun-filled gatherings, on occasion, I would spend entire weekends with Charles and Sally.

My time in the church, however, was not all play! This is the time in my Christian walk when I was challenged to really begin to learn the art of listening, retaining and applying messages preached from the pulpit. Often, on the way home after a service or during a fellowship gathering, Charles would ask me what I had learnt from the most recent sermon, and, at first, my answer would be something simple like "I learnt about Christ"! At the time, I felt that Charles was just out to give me a hard time, asking me questions and upon giving simple answers, making me out to be a fool. As I look back now, I am so thankful for the accountability which I had towards Charles and Sally. Although at first my motive for developing the art of listening was so that I would have a satisfying answer for Charles, had I not been challenged to start exercising my spiritual muscles, I would have missed out on much spiritual growth, a stronger faith and, of course, the joy of experiencing a deeper knowledge of Christ.

The friendship and support of the members of this little Church made the world of difference to me; giving me a sense of self-worth and something to hold on to as I dealt with various difficulties pertaining to life in Green Acres.

Life in the workshop

Living amongst intellectually impaired people was very new to me and I found it extremely difficult to adapt to life in Green Acres. During the day, for the first two months of my stay in the home, I sat in the workshop with all the other residents and day workers. It was hard to accept that there were very few other people with whom one could have a meaningful conversation and it took time for me to get to know each person and their intellectual capabilities. At times, we were kept busy with folding and putting mail into envelopes for large companies who had contracts with the Workshop. Other times, we were kept occupied with various little jobs. Some of these jobs required much fine motor movement such as threading five small safety pins onto one slightly larger safety pin. With the limited use of only one hand, I found this exercise extremely difficult. I was, however, determined to prove that I really wanted to get somewhere in life. Rather than giving up, I took a piece of cotton wool and laid the smaller pins onto it so that it was possible for me to thread them using only one hand. I knew the concept of Matthew 25:21 and I wanted my Father in heaven to say of me: *'Well done, good and faithful servant! You have been faithful with a few things; I will put you in charge of many things...'*

During times when there was nothing to do in the workshop, I tried to keep myself occupied with reading but I could never block out the sounds of senseless arguing and bickering. I often found myself trying to play the role of peacemaker, continually forgetting that these special people have childlike minds and do not have the ability to reason.

During my two months in the workshop, I became well acquainted with a man who was a quadriplegic. Jimmy had broken his neck in a rugby scrum a few years before. He did not have the use of any of his limbs and was dependent on other people for everything, including his ablutions (much to his humiliation). On days when he was strong enough to get up out of bed, he would keep himself busy in the workshop by creating the most beautiful paintings with his mouth. He couldn't understand why God had allowed such a thing to happen to him. Not only was he in a home and totally dependent on others, but he was also isolated from his four beautiful children. Apart from receiving the odd visits from them when they were able to find transport, he no longer had a say in their daily lives. He was angry with God, and he refused to believe that he could find salvation through Christ and even joy in the midst of his trials. Over the years, Jimmy and I shared a good friendship and I was grateful that I had someone in Green Acres with whom I could communicate.

Feathered bundle of joy

A few months after getting to know Jimmy well, I thought that it would be a good idea if we got a little bird and kept it in his room due to the fact that Jimmy spent so much time in bed. This way, his days in bed would not be so dull and empty! Jimmy had a friend whose family bred cockatiels, and before long, we were given a very young little cockatiel. Because my nickname in the home was "Blondie", Jimmy insisted on naming this poor little bird Blondie, after me! In the beginning, Blondie was very wild. Just going near his cage would send him into a wild panic! At the end of each day, when I went to visit Jimmy, I would clean Blondie's cage out and give the bird much attention. Very soon he settled down and even started responding to us. It took a while, but eventually, Blondie became very tame. Blondie soon caught on to the routine, knew when it was time for my afternoon visits and would start calling for me even before I would enter Jimmy's room. Jimmy taught him to whistle and one of his treats was to sit on Jimmy's knee when Jimmy was in his electric wheelchair, and then both of them would ride around the house whistling to each other.

In time, however, Blondie became really noisy, especially when he did not receive attention. So, Jimmy decided that it would be best if Blondie stayed with me in my room. Here, Blondie was in his element because whenever I was in my room, he was out of his cage and happily perched on my shoulder. Considering that Blondie managed to remain on my shoulder despite my poor, shaky walking pattern and all my spasms, I reckon he must have been the most well-balanced cockatiel in the world!

Over the years, Blondie developed so much character! One of his favourite games, which he loved playing while I was busy on the computer, was "hide & seek". He loved hiding behind the computer screen and would get so shy when I "finally" found him. Blondie also loved imitating me typing and would sit on the keyboard, hitting the keys with his beak as fast as he could (I often wondered if he did not give himself a headache) and then would look up at the screen as if he knew exactly what he was typing. He could be quite a pain while

I worked on the computer, especially when he decided to perch on the backspace button!

On a few occasions, Blondie made the great escape and flew away. A couple of times he came very close to death. Each time, I miraculously got him back, but to write about the 'Nine Lives of Blondie' would be a book in itself. Some people may scoff, but I really believe that Blondie was a little gift from my heavenly Father. I went through some very lonely times while in the home, but I always had little Blondie to keep me company and to make me smile.

Sad goodbye

Years later, Jimmy was so weak that his internal organs collapsed and he slipped into a coma. He was in a coma for about 4 days. During this time, I was able to visit him in the hospital once. It was very hard for me to see my dear friend in the state in which he was. I believed that even though in a coma, the chances that he could still hear me were very real. So, I knew that I had to be strong. During my visit, I shared the gospel once again with him, tried to encourage him and prayed for him. I cannot say how I know, but I am certain that he heard everything that I had said to him. Whether he prayed with me, I can only hope. I knew in my heart that this would be the last time that I would see Jimmy and saying goodbye was very hard. The next day, Jimmy passed away.

A chance to prove myself

Before I had moved into Green Acres, I had been promised the opportunity to put my computing skills into practice at the home. After two months of passively sitting in the workshop, I was becoming very restless. *"Was this what life was all about?"* After numerous requests for typing work, and almost making the decision to leave Green Acres and go back to the farm, Trish finally gave me some typing to sit and do for her on the computer in my room. My first assignment was to update the address list of the residents. I was so grateful for the chance to prove myself. Around that time, the secretary who worked for

Trish had resigned, and I was transferred into the office to help out with the typing. At that stage, the government had recently changed power and all documents and forms of Green Acres had to be translated from Afrikaans into English. This became my task. Though I was not paid an official salary, I was given an allowance which was enough to buy my toiletries.

As time went on, I was entrusted with more confidential typing. I was never officially made secretary, as this job description entailed driving around and being a resident of Green Acres, it was not appropriate for me to be involved with the personal and confidential issues of the other residents. I was, however, so very grateful for the fact that I was able to remain in the office and share it with each appointed secretary.   Over the six years that I worked as a typist for Trish, I shared the office with two secretaries. I was so blessed as I had a very good working relationship with each of them. My job in the office made my life in Green Acres so much easier, and I will be forever grateful to Trish for giving me the opportunity to exercise my computing skills and gain so much office experience.

A special friend

About two years after I had moved into Green Acres, I became very good friends with a severely mentally handicapped lady who was also living in the home. As a very difficult person to get along with, Gretha did not have very many friends in the home. Gretha appointed herself as my personal helper, and, for the last four years of my stay in Green Acres, she invested so much of her time in assisting me with whatever help I needed, and for this, I will always be grateful. As with most friendships, this one was not without the occasional eruption. Apart from the fact that I know that if I don't keep myself in check, I can become very demanding, Gretha's inability to reason, and my impatience because of this, often resulted in conflict. I was frustrated by the fact that she would get so worked up over "insignificant" things, and get herself into much unnecessary trouble by fighting with other residents or staff members. Thankfully, it was never too long before the tension blew over and we were laughing again. One of the things that Gretha loved, and insisted on doing, was to pray with me at night before leaving me and going to bed.

A welcome challenge

In 1998, I was granted a bursary by the National Council for Persons with Cerebral Palsy. I took a three-month computer course at Damelin College in Polokwane. This course posed many new challenges for me. During my schooling career and my time at Access College, I had simply been just another disabled student among so many others, with teachers and staff who were all accustomed to disability. Now, however, I was the only disabled student in the class. Although it took a while for the other students to catch on to the fact that it was only my body that was affected by Cerebral Palsy, I was so grateful to my lecturer. She was sensitive to my various needs, such as granting me extra time to complete my exams, and accepting the fact that I could not write my exams by hand, but had to type them on the computer.

Up until this time, ever since I had started using the computer, I had used the old computer operating system, DOS, and I had never used a mouse. Now that I was being taught in Windows, I had to learn how to use the mouse. Due to my spasms and poor fine motor control, learning how to use the mouse was an incredible physical challenge for me. As someone who normally does not easily give up, at first, I did not actually think that I would ever acquire the ability to master the mouse. Classes took place twice a week from five-thirty until eight-thirty in the evenings. Having worked during the day at Green Acres, I found that these three months were a real physical strain on me. Despite all these challenges, by God's grace, and only by God's grace, I was not only able to complete the course and obtain a second diploma, but I also obtained a Merit Award!

Having had a taste of what it was like working in Windows, I found it very frustrating to have to continue working in the old programs. I had acquired more updated computing skills but I was unable to put them to use as our computers at work, as well as my personal computer, were outdated and still running on DOS. Green Acres was not able to afford to buy new, updated computers, so I discussed the possibility of doing fundraising for a new computer for the office. I was prepared to initiate the project. In the meantime, unbeknown to me, Trish had applied for funding from one of the provincial donors and her application had been approved. Upon returning from a short holiday in August 1998, I entered the office and all the staff of Green Acres were waiting to surprise me with my brand-new computer! I was more than overjoyed and there are no words to describe how I felt when I was told that the new computer was actually mine!! And should I ever leave Green Acres, it would go with me! Once again, I was just so amazed at how God had provided for me!

An amazing support system

Towards the end of 1998, for various reasons, our little church dissolved because it was too small and therefore unable to cover the overheads. For a while, I found myself without a place of worship. This time was very unsettling for me. I was living under difficult circumstances and no longer had the security of a church family who knew me, supported me, loved and accepted me just the way I am.

Shirley and Gavin had also been part of our little church, and in fact, I was privileged enough to attend their wedding. A few months after our previous church had closed down, Shirley and Gavin very kindly started fetching and taking me along with them to the Baptist Church, a church much larger than any I had been used to. This time, because the church was so much bigger, it took a little longer for me to settle down and for everyone to get used to the Cerebral Palsied lady. As time went by and I attended various cell groups and fellowship gatherings, more and more people became accustomed to me. Over the years, I have developed many wonderful friendships in this Christ-centred church. Belonging to a larger church and being acquainted with so many more people resulted in me gaining much more self-confidence over time.

There were times during my years in Green Acres when feelings of despair would just overwhelm me. Though very grateful for my job, I was receiving very little payment for my work. I had tried many times to attain higher goals, and, though few exceptions to rules had been made for me (for which I am thankful), I was not given more opportunities to spread my wings and broaden my horizons. I was stuck in my thorny nest! I felt that instead of living life to the full, I was just living a life of day-to-day existence. Also, the thought of living my life this way for the next 25 years or so was a very scary thought to me. Trish fully understood and empathised with my situation, but she was only the social worker and did not have the necessary authority to help me go further.

On the brighter side, I experienced God's provision for me in so many amazing ways during this time! I often received monetary gifts from close friends and many times from anonymous people from within the church. Many times, the money received would be just the correct amount necessary to buy whatever I needed at that time! Very often I would receive a gift, which, at the time of receiving it, I could see no need for. However, I would simply put it away knowing that such gifts were not to be used unwisely. God had impressed it on someone's heart to bless me and it was for a reason. Practically every time this happened, a week or so after receiving the gift, I would become ill and would need to pay for medication, or my glasses would break and I would need to pay for them to be fixed.

Not only did God provide for me financially, but He used so many people from the church to help me in so many different ways. Many of the doctors in different medical fields within the church kindly took me under their care and treated me free of charge. One doctor in particular has been treating me for over ten years now, providing not only his expertise but also medication, refusing to accept payment. During the winter months, I am prone to bronchitis and it has just been such a relief for me to know that I can call on this doctor at any time!

Very often, close friends would arrive at the home with arms full of parcels. They had been out shopping and had just added a "couple of items" to their shopping baskets for me! The parcels contained enough toiletries to last me for more than a month, everything from lovely smelly bath soaps to chocolates. At one time, ants had invaded my room in the home and one holiday, while I was away, a couple from the church kindly had my room fumigated for me. The list of people who assisted me in so many ways is just endless and I am so grateful to each person! God has and continues to use people even outside of the Church to provide for my needs.

One day, I was shopping with a friend in the mall and a young lady came up to us, introducing herself as Kerry. Kerry explained that she was a trainer in horse riding and was very interested in providing horse riding for the disabled. She very kindly said that I would be welcome to go riding with her any time I wanted, free of charge. I was really overwhelmed and knew that this was God's providence. I had not ridden since my days at St Giles and desperately needed the exercise. I have now known Kerry for over twenty years and I have been privileged to enjoy a wonderful friendship with her and her family.

Craig was one of the first friends from church who got to know me well and became a very good friend. He introduced me to a lovely lady by the name of Hayley. Hayley is a hairdresser who has been cutting my hair for almost twenty years now, at no cost. Hayley has always tried her best to make me look and feel good. She does as she pleases with my hair, always ensuring that it is cut in such a way that it is easy for me to manage. Hayley will even highlight my hair at least three times a year. I constantly marvel at how God has taken care of my every need despite my circumstances.

My years at Green Acres and those before were tough, but I am very thankful for those times! Upon leaving college, I would never have imagined that this would be where I'd end up, having studied so hard to make up for my physical limitations. However, according to Psalms 139:16, all the days ordained for me were written before one of them came to be, and even though my plans and ideals had been totally different to what God had planned, I had to accept that His plan for my life was the perfect one and that He really does know what's best for us.

Like the little eaglets, longing for the freedom from their thorny nest, if my early years of adulthood had been easy, if I had not experienced what it was like to start at the bottom with hardly any hope of getting anywhere, or if everything had been handed to me on a silver platter - would I have longed for my independence? Would I have known what it was like to trust God, despite all odds? Would I have had the awesome experience of God's provision in such tangible ways? Would I have learnt so many valuable lessons from the trials which I had experienced? I doubt it! The possibilities are that if my life had been cushioned, padded, protected on every side from struggle and disappointment, I would still be in my comfortable little nest, happy to have a silver spoon shoved in my mouth every time I opened it. However, I truly longed for my freedom!

Baby Debbie

Cuddles with Dad & Mum

Proud sister to her baby brother

Family Portraits

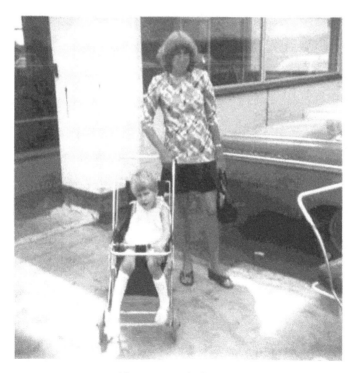

The Future Looked bleak!!!

Trying to gain mobility by learning to ride a bicycle with my feet bandaged to the pedals but this was in vain!

Five months after I began with horse riding, I took my first unaided steps!!!

In 1986, six children from St Giles were selected to go on a fully sponsored trip to England for 3 weeks!

During this trip to the UK, I had the wonderful privilege of meeting my Great Grandmother, my Great Auntie and my Great Uncle Len for the very first time!

My painting, which was chosen to be printed on Christmas cards for disability awareness in 1986

The catch of the day on the great Lake Kariba

My Matric Dance 1993

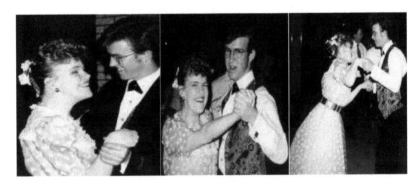

Cristo & Lee's Wedding

Mozambique Outreach – Camp Setting

Mozambique Outreach – Ladies Ministry

Chapter Six:
Tossed in the Turbulence

"Do not be anxious about anything, but in everything, by prayer and petition, with thanksgiving, present your requests to God. And the peace of God, which transcends all understanding, will guard your hearts and minds in Christ Jesus."

— Philippians 4:6-7

There are times in our lives when we go through almost unbearable trials; it is during these times that, like the mother eagle swooping down under her little ones, catching them before they fall to the ground, God graciously carries us through on His almighty wings, giving us the strength to endure and not grow faint.

"He gives strength to the weary and increases the power of the weak. Even youths grow tired and weary, and young men stumble and fall; but those who hope in the LORD will renew their strength. They will soar on wings like eagles; they will run and not grow weary, they will walk and not be faint." Isaiah 40:29-31

— Downward spiral

The following is an account of one of the most difficult times in my life and how my Father God graciously carried me through it.

I had always believed that one day, if I ever got married, I would have a child. Few people supported me in this belief.

However, the general scepticism surrounding this precious dream never dampened my hopes. Why would they? I mean, doctors and specialists had said that I would never walk and my heavenly Father had thrown the spanner in the works, shattering all forms of medical reasoning. By His incomprehensible power, He had enabled me to walk! What on earth was stopping Him from enabling me to have a child?

As I got older, the monthly challenge, faced by all women since Eve, became more and more difficult to cope with. Each month, my body was losing a lot of important minerals which were not being replaced. I would become incredibly tired, and this would result in an increase in my falling. Due to my low immune system at that time of the month, the intensity of my mouth ulcers would increase, resulting in me eating less because of the pain, and I would become even weaker. This was a vicious cycle and was resulting in a downward spiral.

At the age of twenty-three, doctors suggested that I have a hysterectomy. My parents were in favour of this suggestion but they left the final decision entirely up to me, never pressuring me into having the operation and for this, I will always be thankful! I would, however, hear nothing of it! There was no way that I was going to have a hysterectomy. I resented doctors even suggesting the operation. I felt that their reasoning was mainly based on the fact that just because other women with Cerebral Palsy were having the operation at such young ages, I was expected to go with the flow and do the same!

Over the next two years, I put thoughts of the operation out of my mind, not even wanting to think about it!

At the beginning of 1999, a friend made an appointment for me to see her doctor in Polokwane. I was really suffering from my mouth ulcers and I was barely able to eat. We wanted to know if my medication (used to control the convulsions) could not be changed, as Epanutin was a very big contributor to my mouth ulcers. After giving me a check over and asking various questions, much to my irritation, this doctor also recommended that I have a hysterectomy. *"What is it with these doctors? Why such drastic, final measures? Measures, which could not be reversed! Why couldn't I just be given supplements, something to help build me up and help me put on weight?"* The reality was, there was no other alternative. I could not afford to be on supplements for the rest of my life; what would they help anyway, especially as the severity of my problem seemed to be escalating over time? Even after speaking to so many people who encouraged me to think about the possibilities of having the operation, for the better part of that year, I chose once again not to even entertain such thoughts. Trying to ignore my problem, pretend it was not there, I would very often try and hide the fact that my mouth was in so much pain, and, when I'd fallen in private, I would not mention it to anyone. Unfortunately, of course, my falling did not only happen in the privacy of my room! The final straw was when I slipped in the bathroom, bashed my head against the faucet on the side of the toilet, blacked out for a few seconds and suffered a minor concussion.

Pastor Tyler and his precious wife Gigi from the church sat me down one day and in their own special loving way, and made me wake up and face the facts as they really were. I was becoming weaker by the month and in order to be able to give my best in service to the Lord, I needed to take care of my body and ensure that it was healthy and strong. And the fact which was by far the hardest to face, let alone accept, was that bringing up a child would be so very difficult, if not impossible! If I was struggling so much with my own health, how did I expect to cope with giving birth to and bringing up a child as well?

The couple agreed with me fully that with God, anything was possible, but the question that needed to be asked was: *"Is it in God's will for me to have a child?"* As previously mentioned, the ultimate purpose of our existence here on earth is to glorify God and not for selfish gain. Even King David prayed in

Psalm 119:36, *"Turn my heart towards your statutes and not towards selfish gain."* At this point, God was not being glorified in my life. I was seeking selfish gain, not obeying the Lord by seeking His Kingdom first. I was not doing what I needed to, to ensure that my body was healthy so that I could serve Him diligently, and I was not entrusting Him with my own desires.

It was then that I realised how narrow-minded I had been; how I had tried to do things my own way. I am so grateful to the Lord for using this special couple to help me see that I was way out of God's will. I shudder to think what would have happened if I had been left to go my own way, or if I had pressed on in my stubbornness.

My mum and I made the arrangements with my doctor of many years in Duiwelskloof, a little hamlet 70 kilometres from the farm on which my parents lived. The operation was scheduled for the 22nd of November 1999.

During the months leading up to my operation, I received much counsel from so many people from the church. So many rallied around to help me accept the fact that the operation really was necessary. They helped me to work through the reality that I could never have children of my own. I was so anxious about the fact that this operation was so final and we prayed continuously that if it was in fact God's will for me to have children, the operation would not materialise.

Whirlwind of disappointment

A few months before my decision to have the operation, my best friend from school days, Brigetta, announced that she was getting married. Back at school, as most school girls do, we had fantasized about our wedding days. Brigetta had always said that she wanted me to be one of her bridesmaids! However, as Brigetta shared with me the wonderful news of her wedding, she also explained to me that I could not be her bridesmaid because her mother did not think it was appropriate for me as a disabled person to be so involved with the wedding.

She was worried about how the other guests would react towards the Cerebral Palsy. Brigetta's mother's concerns did not faze me, even though Brigetta's family had known me for a long time and I had spent many a weekend with her and her family. I understood how she felt: Many people have never seen a spastic person and are not sure how to react, and so I respected her wishes. I was just glad that I would be at the wedding, sharing in the celebration of Brigetta and her new husband's joyous day, or so I thought!

One Sunday evening five days before the wedding, I received a phone call from Brigetta. I had just returned from spending the afternoon with Gigi in counselling regarding my upcoming operation. We had had a wonderful time of fellowship and I had been given so much encouragement. As I was enthusiastically telling Brigetta that I would be buying my bus ticket that next day, (the wedding was in Pretoria) and asking her if she was feeling nervous about her big day and so on, Brigetta's sombre voice cut through my excited jabber. *"Debbie, you cannot attend my wedding"*.

"What do you mean, Brigetta?" I asked, *"If accommodation is the problem, I can stay with friends in Pretoria!"*

Brigetta explained to me that she and her family had had a huge argument! Though she really wanted me at her wedding, her family did not want me there. They felt that seeing a person like me could be too upsetting for Brigetta's nieces and nephews.

Trying to describe the feelings I felt at that moment is very difficult!

My heart dropped to my feet and my ears were ringing! I could not believe what I was hearing. I was speechless!

"Was I some kind of monster? Is this actually how people see me?"

That night, my prayers to my Heavenly Father were filled with heart-wrenching questions. I could not see the purpose in having to be so different from others and always having to prove to others that I was as normal as anybody else; only my body was different. Neither could I see the reason why

I had to deal with the fact that I would never be a mother to my own child!

My mother was extremely upset by Brigetta's family's attitude towards me and sent her a very strong letter, expressing how deeply we had been hurt as a family. However, as a Christian, even in the midst of heartache, somewhere deep down, I still experienced the blessed assurance that God is Sovereign. He was still in control and nothing takes Him by surprise!

This incident caused my relationship with the Lord to deepen as I realised the value of focusing more on how my Creator and Lord sees me rather than how the world sees me, trusting that He knows what is best for me, and, as so many times before, Romans 8:31 was my source of comfort and strength: *"What, then, shall we say in response to this? If God is for us, who can be against us?"*

Freedom in forgiveness

One year, at our annual Church family camp, our guest speaker placed great emphasis on the importance of forgiveness. I was convicted! Though what had happened was not Brigetta's fault, two years had passed and we had not spoken to each other. After much prayer, I sent Brigetta a letter expressing the fact that I missed her friendship and proposing that we forget what had happened! Brigetta and I were able to work things out and were able to pick up again from where our friendship had left off. Great healing was experienced through forgiveness.

Confirmation through His congregation

During the last two months before my operation, I was so very emotional. As a person who does not easily express emotion publicly, I found myself so often breaking down in tears in the company of close friends during this period in my life. I could not help it; my precious dream of having a child was dying and there was nothing I could do to save it!

All the while, so many continued to pray that God's will would prevail, and for my peace of mind. My church family did so much more than just lift me up in prayer and offer me their counsel. The Saturday before I left Polokwane for my operation, which was to be performed in Duiwelskloof, my close friend from church, Irmela, kindly arranged for me to be treated to a manicure and pedicure during the morning. That afternoon we had to be at the church for a ladies' tea, at which a guest speaker from America, the author Mary Summerville, was going to be addressing us. After a lovely tea, we all settled down in the sanctuary to listen to the speaker. On the table in front was a glass containing three roses. One was for the eldest lady in the group, the second was for our guest speaker, and the third, much to my surprise, was for me! I was called up and seated on a chair in front, facing the ladies. A parcel so big that I could barely hold it was placed in my lap. Our senior pastor's wife read a few verses to me from the Bible and then I was committed to the Lord in prayer.

The Sunday before, I had gone home for Cristo's 21st birthday celebration, and in my absence, during the morning service, the congregation as a whole was informed of my upcoming operation and was encouraged to pray for me. It was also mentioned that the ladies were planning to get a few gifts together and show their love and support for me by blessing me during the ladies' tea that next Saturday afternoon. An invitation was extended to anyone wishing to contribute by way of a card or gift.

There are just no words to describe how I felt that Saturday afternoon as I was saturated by the love and support of my church family. The parcel contained everything I needed for my stay in hospital from sleepwear, cosmetics, perfume, a vanity case, to a walkman and so much more. Included were gift vouchers for clothing as well as enough cash to pay for my whole operation! I was later told that throughout the previous week, church members (even the men) had been dropping gifts off at Bev's house for me. Chris and Bev have been very close friends to me since I joined Christ Baptist Church. I was truly overwhelmed by the love of God, which was reaching out to me through His children. *Was this amazing provision God's way of showing me that*

I was not making a mistake by having the operation? The more I pondered this question, the more peace I began to experience. I mean, after so much prayer for God's guidance, would He really leave me to go ahead and have the operation if it were His plan for me to bear my own children? *"If any of you lacks wisdom, he should ask God, who gives generously to all without finding fault, and it will be given to him."* James 1:5

No turning back

I went home to the farm on Friday the 18th of November and on Monday the 21st, I was admitted to the quaint little public hospital in Duiwelskloof, which is surrounded by mountains. I was grateful to be in this hospital, as, unlike most other provincial hospitals, it was small, very clean, and all the staff were very friendly, taking a genuine personal interest in their patients' wellbeing and comfort.

Sharing the room with me was another lady who was in for minor surgery, and who would be discharged the next day. She was also a Christian. After the nurses had finished preparing me for the next day's surgery, and the doctor had been to see me and we had all settled down for the night, the two of us experienced an unforgettable evening of sharing memory verses with each other. Meditating upon God's Word just filled me with peace that truly transcended all understanding. I was amazed at how peacefully I slept that night, despite the fact that the next day was the day that I had been dreading for so many months; in fact, years!

Surgery went well, but was not without complication. When my parents came to visit me that evening, Dad told me just how seriously I had needed the operation. According to the doctor, as they started the surgery, they were not able to find my womb. As a result of my walking pattern, my womb had shifted and had been lying against my spine. Because of its position, my womb had not been able to drain properly and was therefore not only very mushy and pulpy but three times its normal size!

As a result, I could have developed cancer of the womb. A pregnancy could have resulted in me becoming paralyzed! Did I need more confirmation that I had done the right thing? The relief of knowing that I had not made an irreversible mistake just flooded over me like cool spring water bringing with it feelings of such joy and thankfulness in my heart towards my Sovereign Father in heaven. He truly is in control of our lives at all times, even when it does not feel that way! *"Many are the plans in a man's heart, but it is the Lord's purpose that prevails."* Proverbs 19:21

I don't understand why God chose not to enable me to have children of my own. I know that anything is possible for our Heavenly Father. By His great and mighty Power, He could have prevented my womb from getting into the state in which it was. Yes, it would have been hard, but with the Power of the Holy Spirit, we would have found a way to overcome each obstacle as it arose.

I do, however, accept and honour the fact that this was not part of His perfect plan for me. A big part of me is grateful to Him for the fact that I will not be having the stress of such a huge physical challenge and responsibility resting upon my shoulders. The other part of me that sometimes still mourns the fact that I will never know what it feels like to hold my own baby, knows that the deep, intense love inside of me, which I would have given to my own child, can be expressed towards other little ones in the church and especially to those who do not necessarily experience the love and guidance of a Christian mother.

No matter how deep was the desire for my own children, my desire for the Lord to have His Way and for Him to be glorified in my life is far greater!

Divine appointment

I spent six weeks at home on the farm, recovering from surgery. Even this time at home was part of God's Sovereign plan. His timing is so perfect. Six days after my surgery, I was still in bed and barely able to get up when Bill, my dad's boss, was gruesomely murdered. Responding to a call for help over the farm emergency radio from his wife Vera, at 06:00 am, my dad was the first to reach their house, just 2 kilometres from our own home. As Vera was coming out of the house and as Dad was walking up the path to meet her, they simultaneously saw Bill's lifeless body lying in the garage. He had been shot twice and stabbed about 20 times.

This was an extremely traumatic time for us as a family, but especially for Dad!

Often, Gigi, Bev and other members of my church family unselfishly made the two-hour journey from Polokwane to the farm to see me. These visits made the world of difference, not only to me but also to my parents as they were also ministered to. I praise God for His divine providence *"For in him we live and move and have our being..."* Acts 17:28

After my operation, I felt like a different person. I definitely had much more energy and it is such a pleasure not to have to experience all the pain and fatigue which I had so regularly experienced before having the operation.

A great honour

Just over a year after my operation, my good friends, Craig and Irmela, decided to get married. I was asked to be one of Irmela's bridesmaids. Being asked to be a bridesmaid was such an honour for me and it took a while for the reality of it to sink in, especially after the experience I had had with Brigetta. At first, I thought that Irmela had asked me on the spur of the moment without putting much thought into the implications. So, I asked Irmela to think about it and make sure that she knew what she was in for if she had me as one of her bridesmaids. I would hardly be able to assist her with anything in preparation for or on her big day. Instead of me helping her into her dress and with her make-up, I needed help with these things myself! I would not be able to follow her around, and be at her every beck and call on her wedding day as is the normal role of a bridesmaid. It was just inconceivable to me that Irmela wanted me to be her bridesmaid in light of what had happened with Brigetta's wedding.

Without hesitation, Irmela insisted that she wanted me as one of her bridesmaids and that all of the above mentioned were of no concern to her.

Irmela's wedding day was a very special day and although all responsibility of being a bridesmaid rested on Irmela's other bridesmaids' shoulders, the experience of leading Irmela down the aisle on her wedding day was truly an unforgettable one for me.

Each individual has to face their unique share of trials. Some trials can really throw us into absolute turmoil and desperation but praise God for His promise in James 1:2-4; "*Consider it all joy, my brethren, when you encounter various trials knowing that the testing of your faith produces endurance. And let endurance have its perfect result, so that you may be perfect and complete, lacking in nothing.*"

Although, at times, various trials have almost thrown me off course, clinging to this great promise as well as many others in the Bible has enabled me to endure many trials. After all, Philippians 1:6 says that it is God who will complete the work that He has begun in me. I am so grateful that my continued relationship with the Lord does not depend on my good works. I have truly been blessed with a deeper knowledge of our Lord and Saviour as a result of these trials.

> *Have mercy on me, my God, have mercy on me, for in you I take refuge. I will take refuge in the shadow of your wings until the disaster has passed.*
>
> — Psalm 57:1

Chapter Seven:
Waiting to Take Wind

"Wait for the LORD; Be strong and let your heart take courage; Yes, wait for the LORD."

— **Psalm 27:14**

It is vital for an eagle to find enough food to satisfy its minimum energy requirements. Most eagles spend a good deal of their time resting. Resting serves to conserve valuable energy and also relates to their dependence on the winds. Eagle hunters must wait to take wind until the air has warmed enough to create the rising air currents, or thermals, that they need. The heavier the eagle, the later in the day it begins to hunt.

At times in our lives, it is not easy to see the hand of God in our circumstances. All we can see is the here and now. All we can feel is pain, helplessness and sometimes, even desperation. Despite the way we feel, we need to cling to the promise of Romans 8:28; *"And we know that in all things, God works for the good of those who love him, who have been called according to his purpose."* If we love Him, we need to believe that God is actually using our suffering for our good and for His glory as we will see in this chapter.

Unfulfilled existence

I lived and worked at Green Acres for 6 years. However, as time went by, I became anxious and unsettled. I felt as if I was not living life to my fullest potential. Though I worked from eight in the morning to three-thirty in the afternoon, I felt as if I was not getting anywhere in life. After six years of trying desperately to prove myself, I was still seen as a resident of Green Acres, merely being kept occupied with typing.

My goal had been to become a staff member, to receive a salary, and to even become exempt from all the restrictions of the home. I did not see myself as better than the other residents but I had goals in life. Most of the other residents were intellectually impaired and unperturbed about sitting in the workshop, sometimes being kept busy with handwork, other times doing nothing. Where the intellectually impaired needed so much supervision and discipline, I had the capacity to think and to take responsibility for myself. However, for the sake of fairness, everyone in Green Acres was treated equally; very few exceptions to the rules were made for a person who is not intellectually impaired. I had worked so hard to excel at school and college, not because I wanted to be better than others, but because I knew that if I wanted to get anywhere in life, I would have to compensate for my disability.

"Was all that hard work for nothing? Was this where I was going to be for the rest of my life?"

If I was going to have to stay at Green Acres for the rest of my life, then I needed to trust that this was God's plan for my life. I needed to stop bemoaning my situation. I needed to rest in Him and be open to what He wanted to teach me through my stay in Green Acres, however long that would be.

By God's grace and His leading, I started a Bible study. I taught God's Word on a very simple level to an average of ten to fifteen mostly intellectually impaired adults, for four years. I will always remember the absolute pleasure that these people got out of singing praises to God. Although it was very difficult to ascertain their spiritual growth due to behavioural problems, and at times, I became very discouraged, I knew that it was God's will that I should persevere. Only one day, in heaven, will we see the fruits hereof.

For one year I gave computer lessons to nine mainly intellectually impaired adults. I had to put my own curriculum together and divided it into elementary and intermediate levels, as some of my students had a higher intellectual capacity than others. I also had to translate my lessons into Afrikaans as most of my students were Afrikaans-speaking. The computer course included tests and exams, just like a real course. At the end of the year, each student was presented with a certificate at the year-end function of the home. Yes, this was hard work for me and I knew that the possibility of these students actually retaining and using their computer skills was very slim, but the fact that they derived much pleasure and, more importantly, stimulation from these lessons, made it worth all the time and effort.

One year, I was the director of the recreational committee of Green Acres. My main objective for the committee was to organise recreational activities for the residents that would provide enjoyment and stimulation. I ran a little snack shop, which I opened twice a week. The profit it made would go into buying games, hiring videos for the residents to watch over weekends, and organising outings. I put together a tri-monthly little magazine that included simple biblical messages, articles on birds or trees which were common to the grounds of Green Acres, articles on various achievements by people in the home, and competitions. Most importantly, I encouraged the residents of Green Acres, as well as the day workers of the workshop, to write their own little articles for the magazine.

A highlight for me that year was the jailbird dance which we organised. I had such fun helping with organising it, especially as I knew that there was hardly anything that the people of Green Acres enjoyed more than a dance. Everyone had to dress up as either policemen, policewomen, or prisoners. There was a prize for the best-dressed couple, and boy, were there some sights to see! Dinner was stew and rice; the only cutlery used was plastic spoons. We decorated the windows of the workshop with paper on which jail bars had been painted. The Polokwane Police Station lent us a "mini jail" which was a huge cage, with four scummy-looking beds inside, which we placed at the entrance to the dance. This attracted much curiosity and excitement amongst the residents and day workers. I was so blessed to see the participation and enjoyment that evening.

At the end of that year, I resigned as director and the recreational committee was dissolved. I found that due to the limitations of the other committee members, most of what was involved was resting heavily upon me and I was beginning to feel the physical strain.

Despite my endeavours to make the best of my situation, I still could not make peace with the fact that living in Green Acres was possibly where I would be for the rest of my life. I had always felt that the Lord had something more in store for me. In the back of my mind, I had always had the idea of myself living and working outside the boundaries of the home. Out of the goodness of their hearts, many people counselled me not to think this way; to try and accept my circumstances and to be grateful for what I had. I tried to do this, and, to a greater extent, I managed to convince myself that I would not be able to live and work within a "normal" environment. However, I still could not see myself living out the next 25 years or so of my life in Green Acres. I commented once to a faithful friend and mentor saying, "The only way I'll ever get out of the home is if some poor sucker decides to sweep me off my feet and marry me". Her response was, "Debbie, do not put your faith in man, but in God". What sound advice that was, even though at the time, I could not see how God would take me out of Green Acres without sending that "poor sucker". I had to wait six years before what I thought were rock-solid walls turned into dust as God, by His great Sovereignty, drastically changed my circumstances.

We have to be so careful not to put limitations on God. We don't see the big picture, but God, the Creator of the universe, does. Why wouldn't He? He created the heavens and the earth and everything in the earth. How can we ever think that we can figure Him out and manipulate Him into doing what we think is right and should be done in our lives?

"You turn things around! Shall the potter be considered as equal with the clay, That what is made would say to its maker, "He did not make me"; Or what is formed say to him who formed it, "He has no understanding"?

— Isaiah 29:16b

Chapter Eight:
Homing In on the Catch

"Therefore, since we have so great a cloud of witnesses surrounding us, let us also lay aside every encumbrance of sin which so easily entangles us, and let us run with endurance the race that is set before us, fixing our eyes on Jesus, the author and perfector of faith, who for the joy set before Him endured the cross, despising the shame, and sat down at the right hand of the throne of God"

— **Hebrews 12:1-2**

African fish eagles can catch prey over ten times their own body weight. If it is too heavy to allow the eagle to get lift, it drags the fish across the surface of the water until it reaches the shore. When it catches a fish which is too heavy to allow the eagle to sustain flight, it will drop into the water and paddle to the nearest shore with its wings.

It was over six years since that conversation with my dear friend when I found myself sitting in my own cosy little flat, writing about God's faithfulness in my life, with a wonderful job at a school, outside of the boundaries of Green Acres!

Divine opportunity

How did all this happen? I believe God was already laying the foundations back in 1998, four years before. A few months before, a friend had asked me to share my testimony with the ladies of a Christian Ladies' Club. A pastor's wife from another church in town was also a guest speaker at this meeting and a few weeks after hearing my testimony, she invited me to share my testimony at a ladies' evening, held at a motel in town.

It is always a great joy for me to share my testimony; not only are others so encouraged but I am always reminded afresh of how intimately involved the Creator of this universe has continuously been in my own life! When I had accepted the invitation, I had not realised how grand the occasion was. Nor had I realised just how many ladies I would be addressing. Everything in the dining room was so beautifully laid out and there were about one hundred ladies, all dressed in their lovely evening wear. We were served a three-course meal, and, to top it all, I was seated at the head table! I truly felt inadequate for the task. *"What did I have to say that would be of any benefit to these ladies? Would they even be able to understand my speech?"* Throughout the meal, I prayed that our dear Lord would help me speak clearly and that the ladies would be encouraged upon hearing how God had worked in my life. The Lord was truly with me that night and I was so thankful that the ladies had seemed to understand me and had even been blessed in many ways by what I had shared.

Quite often since then, when I meet ladies in town, they comment "I know Debbie, I heard her testimony". This leaves me with such a feeling of accountability. There are ladies out there who know me but are strangers to me. Do they see God being glorified in my life or have they been left with a feeling of disappointment? My prayer is that we, as Christians, would not just talk the talk but seriously walk the walk, by God's strength.

Ultimate frustration

In January of 2002, my feelings of frustration came to a head. I knew that there was something more to my existence than living such a stifled life in Green Acres. I just did not know what that "something more" was! One Sunday evening, at our prayer meeting before the evening service, much to my embarrassment, I broke down in tears. I just could not see an end to my frustrations. My little finite mind could imagine no alternative other than life in Green Acres. That evening, our pastor and many others lifted me up in prayer. God's timing is amazing, His Word says: "*No temptation has overtaken you but such as is common to man; and God is faithful, who will not allow you to be tempted beyond what you are able, but with the temptation will provide the way of escape also, so that you will be able to endure it.*" 1 Corinthians 10:13.

I knew that God was still in control. Just when I was feeling so desperate, grappling with the fact that maybe this was where I should be and trying to make peace with it, the prayers of my brothers and sisters were answered and doors that I never imagined even existed flew open!

Glimmer of light at the end of the tunnel

Kerry, from horse riding, was speaking to me on the phone one evening. Knowing me the way she does, it did not take her long to realise something of the struggle which was taking place inside of me. She spoke to a friend of hers whose brother-in-law owned a school in town and the very next day she phoned me to tell me that I had an interview at a private school, accommodating over 3,000 children. I was so very grateful to Kerry and her friend for organising the interview for me, although, deep down, I did not feel positive about it. Understandably, when strangers meet me for the first time, they are prone to think that I am not capable of much due to the severity of my disability. This is due to a lack of knowledge regarding disabled people. Ever since I can remember, I have made it my responsibility to educate the people I meet informally, using much humour, teaching them that I, as a disabled person, am just as capable of engaging in intelligent conversation, having fun, feeling the feelings that everyone else feels and even participating in much of what everyone else does, though maybe a bit slower or by way of other means. However, this takes time and during an interview, it is not possible. No matter how glossy one's CV or how many glowing references one might have to one's name, if the interviewer does not have an open mind towards a disabled person, to the interviewer, "*what you see is what you get*"; his mind is made up, and you don't get the job! I had already been to a few interviews in the past and this is what I had experienced. In fact, a couple of times I have walked out of an interview actually feeling dumb because this is the way that I had been treated. However, I make a point of trying not to take this kind of treatment personally because I am aware that the average person is not well-informed about people with disabilities, and that this kind of treatment is all as a result.

Despite my negative feelings towards my interview, I really prayed and also asked friends for much prayer. I was reminded of all the mind-blowing accounts in the Old Testament of how God had provided for and preserved His nation, the Israelites. Just look at the accounts of Ruth and Esther and one's mind is already overwhelmed by God's love and dedication to His people. Is our Father just the God of miracles in the Bible? Or does He perform miracles today in the lives of His children? He is our Father: *"Or what man is there among you who, when his son asks for a loaf, will give him a stone? Or if he asks for a fish, he will not give him a snake, will he? If you then, being evil, know how to give good gifts to your children, how much more will your Father who is in heaven give what is good to those who ask Him!"* Matthew 7:9-11. What was stopping Him from doing a miracle in my situation if, of course, it was part of His Sovereign plan for my life?

What you see is NOT what you get

A miracle is exactly what our Father performed that Tuesday morning when I walked into the principal's office for the interview! As I entered the office, the principal exclaimed, "*I know Debbie; I heard her testimony four years ago at the ladies' evening*". How is that for Divine Intervention? The principal was already aware of my background, she had already heard all of how God had worked in my life and she already knew that I was capable of more than what meets the eye! I began to feel very positive as I was given a Grade 12 mathematical paper to take home and type as a typing test. A week later, the principal called and invited me to a second interview. She explained that someone was needed to be available in the school uniform shop throughout the morning. I would need to sell uniforms to parents and children and, in addition to selling uniforms, I would be required to assist teachers with the typing of tests and exams when necessary. There were question marks in both of our minds as to whether I would be able to handle the job. The typing was not a problem for me, but the questions were: How would the parents and children react to my disability? Would they understand my speech? Would I be too slow in serving customers? Would I cope in a normal working environment? Despite all these unspoken questions, at the end of our conversation, the principal encouraged me with these words: *"Debbie, we'll never know if we don't try!"* If only more people could have such an attitude!!

Marietjie, an Occupational Therapist who is also a close friend, accompanied me to my second interview. We all really appreciated Marietjie's contribution that day. She explained more about my disability and gave practical advice with regard to overcoming obstacles, which would have been physical challenges to me in my working environment. I would start working the following week, with Sonja as my supervisor.

I could not have asked for better working hours. I easily become physically tired, and God is more aware of this than anyone else and so He took care of this minor problem. In order to ensure that I can always give my best, He blessed me with a job where I would only work half a day and I got to enjoy school holidays.

As Jeremiah said to the Israelites during the Babylonian captivity; *"For I know the plans that I have for you,' declares the LORD, 'plans for welfare and not for calamity to give you a future and a hope."* Jeremiah 29:11

Early days in the open labour market

During the first two weeks at work, I had to face some of the biggest challenges of my life. After having been dropped off on my first day, on my way walking from the car to the office, I was followed by about twenty to thirty primary school children, laughing and chanting. They did not know better. Most of them had probably never seen a person affected by Cerebral Palsy before. Traditionally, in the African culture, disabled people are kept at home. They are very often not included in society and in some cultures, people like me are sometimes associated with witchcraft. As I finally reached the office, I was shaken, wondering if I would indeed be able to settle down and cope in a normal working environment. Was I being unrealistic and had I fooled myself into thinking that I could cope? As I entered the office, I challenged myself with this thought; *"Debbie, you can either walk in here in tears or you can hold your head up high and know in your heart that God does not make mistakes. He made you. He has a purpose and it is only through His strength that there could be any chance of you making it in this job"*. I made my choice and was so grateful that God had reminded me that He was in control.

During the weeks that followed, Sonja coached and encouraged me. I believe that a major part of my success is due to the fact that Sonja believed in me. Despite there being so many things with which I battled physically, such as handling the cash box with its small key, locking and unlocking the shop, and even battling with small change due to my spasticity, Sonja believed in me even when, at times, I doubted myself. As time went on, I developed my own unique way of doing things and eventually, I was able to handle the cash box, including the small change and much more. By God's grace, I taught myself how to use the accounting program, which is the main computer program I used in my job.

As I adjusted to working in a normal working environment, I found that I was able to do more than what was originally expected. Running the stationery shop became an added responsibility. This entailed taking stock of stationery, fortnightly making up teachers' stationery orders, and processing the orders through the computer.

In the beginning, teachers and other members of staff were very uncertain as to how to react to my disability. So, instead of coming directly to me and asking about anything concerning uniforms or stationery, they would walk the whole school in search of Sonja. Sonja played such an active role in educating my co-workers and helping them to understand that I was in fact capable of assisting them. When they finally found Sonja and made their enquiries, she would simply tell them that I was now working in that department and that they needed to ask me for whatever they needed.

Eventually, I enjoyed a wonderful relationship with most students and staff.

My disability did limit some of the physical aspects of the job. I always battled to unlock and lock the shop. I was unable to lift and carry boxes. At times when the shop was extra busy, I was not quick enough in helping all the customers within a limited amount of time. I was unable to do stock-taking on my own because some of the clothes were unreachable or in boxes. To assist me with these things, I was given a wonderful helper, Rahab, who not only cleaned the shops, but was there to assist me when necessary. I was so very grateful to my supervisors for this providence and I viewed this as such a wonderful example of accommodating a disabled person in the workplace!

Primitive ground explored

Eight months after I started working at the school, I began thinking about the possibilities of moving into one of the flats on the school premises, which are available to staff at the school. At first, I dismissed the idea in my mind as impossible. I would not allow myself to even think about it. Once again, so many people with good intentions tried to encourage me to accept the fact that I could not cope on my own in a flat. I had to make peace with the fact that I would have to live in a home for the rest of my life. I really wanted to make that peace, but I felt so bound by the rules and regulations of Green Acres. Having gone to boarding school during the whole of my schooling career, I could not help wondering what it would be like to be able to live a life free of rules. What would it be like to have a personal bathroom? What would it be like to be able to get up on a Saturday morning when I wanted to? What would it be like to be able to come and go as I pleased? In summary, what would it be like to be able to just live life the way an adult person blessed with a sound mind should be able to live life?

Tanja, a colleague of mine at the time, occupied one of these flats at the school. Tanja and I had many conversations, discussing all the implications involved with me moving out of Green Acres and into my own flat! We would sit and work out solutions to what would have been problems for me living on my own. We would need to have the bath taken out and a shower put in, as getting in and out of the bath on my own would be too dangerous. I would pay a cleaner to do my washing, ironing and all the heavy work for me. I would not need to cook for myself as I would be able to eat out of the hostel kitchen. If need be, I would be able to make a light meal for myself in the microwave. Throughout each day, as I faced everyday physical challenges, I would ask myself, *"what would I do if I was on my own in my flat and this situation arose?"* Then, by God's grace, I would work out a solution to that challenge. I began to feel more and more that living on my own could be possible as I thought through my everyday routine and evaluated the amount of help that I really needed.

Still convinced deep down that I was living in a dream world, I searched for the counsel of professional people who had often worked with me and knew me well. I was hoping that they would talk some sense into me and help me see that it was in fact impossible for me to live on my own. First, I spoke to Marietjie, the occupational therapist. Marietjie listened as I shared my dream. She was very realistic with me and asked questions: What I would do when I got sick? What about assistance, which may be needed at unexpected times?

Together, we discussed these questions. Together, we searched for answers. By the end of our meeting, I was beginning to feel as if maybe this idea of occupying a flat at the school was a possibility. I then spoke to Carol, the wife of one of our pastors. After sharing with her my desire and explaining the possibilities to her, instead of sitting me down and trying to explain why it would not be possible, she left me with these words, *"Debbie, I dare you to go for it."* I was speechless. I really appreciated the support and prayers of many close brothers and sisters in the church.

By God's grace, I had everything worked out and by God's grace, I had found ways to overcome obstacles that would have made it very difficult for me to live on my own. What was the next step? The next step was the hardest; it was to lay my plans before my parents and obtain their blessing to move out of Green Acres and become independent. My parents, especially my dad, would not even think about the possibility of me living on my own. Ever since I can remember, Dad would explain to me that there was just no way! How would I cook for myself? What if I had a fall with a kettle full of boiling water in my hand? What if I had a fall and cracked my head open with nobody around to help? How I love my parents for their love and concern! However, this would be different; I would not be living totally on my own, as there would be people all around. This would not be a situation where I would be totally isolated from people and would have to completely fend for myself. I would be living on my own; independent, able to experience and enjoy life as any adult person with a normal brain does, but still within a semi-sheltered environment!

I spent time with my parents over the December holidays and after much prayer, I gently shared my plans with my dad. I had already told Mum, and, after explaining all the possibilities to her, she was even excited! Dad listened and asked questions, questions that I had asked myself so many months before and had been blessed with the answers. *"Dad, my plan is to have the bath removed and a shower put in. My meals will be cooked for me. I will pay one of the cleaners to clean, to do my washing and ironing as well as to give me any assistance that I may need while she is busy in the flat".*

The more I shared the possibilities with my dad, the more open he became to the idea and by the end of the holiday, I had my parents' support. If the school committee agreed to allow me to occupy one of the flats, and if I complied with various conditions laid down by my dad with regards to my safety, they would give me their blessing.

Finally, I needed to approach school management and find out whether they would in fact be prepared to take the chance and agree to allow me to live in the next flat that became available.

At the beginning of January, Sonja came and had tea with me in celebration of my birthday. I had no intention of making my request known to Sonja just then, but as we were alone with no staff or telephone to interrupt, I felt that it was a good time to approach the subject. I must admit that I really did not think that it would be easy to convince Sonja that I could manage with living on my own, but not long into the conversation, Sonja exclaimed *"Yes, Debbie, I personally have been thinking of the possibility for quite a while"*. This was such an encouragement to me to know that, once again, I had her support in what would thus far be the biggest step towards independence in my life. We had such an awesome time discussing all the details regarding my possible move. At the end of our tea, I knew that I was one step closer to realising my dream.

Even before we were certain that I would get the flat, a very good friend of mine so kindly put aside a whole lot of furniture for my little flat. Her family was emigrating to Ireland at the time. We stored the furniture in Pastor Dave and Carol's garage, not quite sure whether I would ever actually get the privilege of using it.

During February, Tanja announced that she was moving out of her flat. This meant that soon there would be a flat available. At that time, I had heard that there was a strong possibility that I would not get the flat, as there was genuine concern from the school committee about my safety. Although I appreciated this concern, I felt so very disappointed. Even in my deep disappointment, though, I knew that God was still sovereign and He was still in control. He was still at the wheel, steering me through life's incredible journey not only over mountain tops covered with beautiful trees, and fresh streams with breathtaking views of His amazing grace, but also through dry, lonely deserts where you can see no end to the hot desert sand, and there seems to be no meaning to the situation in which you find yourself; no meaning to life; all for reasons carrying the weight of eternal blessing. Those reasons: to teach me to trust in Him, to show His power through my weaknesses and ultimately, to make me more like His precious Son. I had been working on a letter of motivation to hand over to the school's management committee asking for a flat and explaining to them in full detail how I intended to make it work, by God's grace. Melanie, a very good friend, encouraged me to complete the motivation letter and hand it into the school even though I was convinced that I would not get the flat. I completed my motivation and handed it in on the Wednesday after much prayer. On Friday, just two days later, I received an answer from the school owner and the management committee of the school: I could have the flat! Not only could I have a flat, but one of the teachers would be asked to move out of his flat and into Tanja's old flat. Why? Because his flat had a shower! It turned out that this flat was much more practical for me than Tanja's flat would have been. It was open plan, much easier to clean. The toilet and shower area were very small and so it was almost impossible for me to have a fall. At times, I felt as if this flat was built just for me!

The big move

My parents came to pick me up for the April school holidays and I took them to see the flat. Understandably, Dad was beginning to have his doubts! This was such a big step. *Were we being realistic? Were we making a mistake? What would happen if I moved out of Green Acres, lost my place and found that I could not cope after all?* I would have to go and live with my parents on the farm and there I would be worse off than what I was at the home because I would not have a job, nor would I have the kind of church life which I had here in Polokwane. I would not have a social life! *"Why don't we just play it safe, rather than taking the chance? Let's be grateful for what we have and make the best of it."* I know that this is how Dad felt because at times I felt the same, but something inside me just could not, would not let the opportunity of having a taste of independence slip through my fingers.

When I was finally able to show my parents the flat, it was almost as if a light switch was flipped on; I was amazed at how they instantly fell in love with the flat! The security of the flat was a great relief to them: not only did I have an outside gate, I also had a security gate and the windows were fully burglar-barred. The flat was almost three times the size of the room which I had at Green Acres. They loved the little kitchen area, not to mention the bathroom area; in short, it was perfect! As we drove home to the farm that afternoon, the feeling of joy, excitement and anticipation inside of me was just too overwhelming. There was so much to do. That evening, we sat out in the lapa (courtyard), my mum with pen in hand, making out lists of everything that I would need for my little flat. I went to bed that night with a feeling of such awe towards my Father in heaven. Yes indeed: *"Looking at them, Jesus said, "With people it is impossible, but not with God; for all things are possible with God.""* Mark 10:27

The April school holidays were only two weeks long. During this time, we would have to make another trip to Polokwane for an appointment with the principal in order to finalise my move, and thereafter, an appointment at Green Acres in order to give notice.

The Hand of God was in this whole project from beginning to end! Our appointment with the principal was such a blessing. My parents assured her that should the time come where I would no longer be able to look after myself, they or (if they were no longer able to) other family members would take the responsibility of moving me out of the flat and back into a place where I would receive the necessary care. Finally, the time came to ask the question which was weighing rather heavily on all three of our minds: "How much would I have to pay for rent?" My total income was minimal and therefore we knew that if more than what I was able to afford was required for rent, I would not be able to make the move! Dad asked the question.   In reply, the principal just casually dismissed the idea and said that personnel staying in the flats were not required to pay rent nor did they have to pay for their meals! This was almost too much for me to comprehend! Jehovah Jireh truly is my great provider! For my accommodation in Green Acres, my parents had to make a monthly financial contribution in addition to what I was paying out of my Disability Grant. Now, not only would I be able to afford to move, but I would be totally financially independent of my parents. Yet another dream of mine was about to be realised!

Our appointment with the director of Green Acres was also very fruitful! Under normal circumstances, when a resident leaves Green Acres, a month's notice must be given. I was planning to move out within the next week, the 4th of April. Paying accommodation for the whole of the month of April went without saying in my mind! However, nobody (including myself) was one hundred percent certain that I would really cope living independently. After discussing these concerns, the director of the home suggested that I try it for two weeks; if, after two weeks, I found that I was not coping, I was welcome to move back into the home. If by the 19th of April, I was sure that I could manage, my room would be given to the next person on the waiting list. Did this mean that I would also have to pay accommodation for the month of May as well if I had decided by the 19th that I was coping? In reply, I was told that if somebody moved into my old room by the 1st of May, it would not be necessary. I was really very grateful for the exceptions which had been made for me.

The following week was filled with long shopping lists and trips to town. When I reflect back on that time, I am so awestruck at how God so gracefully provided everything I needed. A few years earlier, the cell group which I was attending decided to bless me by purchasing a microwave for me. While in Green Acres, I did not make full use of it but little did we all know that a few years down the line, it would be one of the most essential appliances that I would need in my flat. My fridge cost me R200; my chest of drawers cost me

R300. All in all, everything I needed for the flat (kitchenware, bathroom appliances, a new bed, etc.), as well as everything my dad needed in order to do necessary maintenance, which included putting up an outside light for me and making special adaptations here and there, cost me a mere R2000. I was blessed with everything else which I needed by my brothers and sisters in the church who surprised me with a house-warming party a few weeks after moving into my flat.

The fourth of April 2003 was a day never to be forgotten! We left the farm that morning in two bakkies (pick-up trucks), my mum and I in one and three farmworkers in the other; Dad was to follow later. Having offloaded the bakkies at the flat, we collected the furniture which had been so graciously given to me from storage. After that followed the horrifying task of packing and moving everything out of my room at Green Acres. Though my room was so small, I still got rid of boxes and boxes of stuff that I did not use and clothes that I did not wear. I still have no idea how I managed to store the amount of rubbish which I had accumulated over the six years at Green Acres!

My parents stayed with me on the Friday and Saturday nights, something which was not possible while I was living in the home! While Dad was sorting out my electrical appliances, putting up an outside light, hanging pictures and doing odd jobs, Mum helped me unpack boxes. My parents worked so hard that weekend, helping me to get settled into my little flat. I really prayed that it was not all for nothing, that in two weeks' time I would not have to move back into Green Acres.

I had two weeks in which I would have to find someone who would be prepared to clean my flat and do my washing and ironing and basically, to settle down into a routine. Within the first day of school starting, Monday the 7th of April 2002, Sonja and I had finalised all the finer details. I would be taken to and from work in my wheelchair as the distance between the school shops and my flat was too far for me to walk. Under normal circumstances, everyone must have their meals in the dining room but because the dining room is so far for me to walk, my food would be sent to my flat. This meant that I could warm my meals up in my microwave and eat whenever I was ready to eat. On that same day, Rahab, the lady who assisted me at work, agreed to work for me in my flat after hours! I could not have asked for a better helper. Everything she did was done with such dedication. Rahab was so familiar with all my needs that most of the time before I had even asked her to help me with anything, she had already done it. Rahab was more than my helper; she was a precious friend and a gift from God.

At first, I found it difficult to settle down into a routine. I found that by the end of each day, I was exhausted. Much of my tiredness was because I was so determined that I was going to make it on my own, that I ended up trying too hard and putting much needless pressure on myself. I soon learnt that I was not on my own after all, and relying heavily on the assistance of our Heavenly Father became very much part of everyday life for me. Even simple things such as carrying a jug of milk without spilling it, or doing up an especially difficult button and so much more, would not have been possible for me if I did not have the loving, supernatural help of the Holy Spirit.

As I learnt to rest in Him, by the end of my first two weeks, I was able to inform the home that I would not be returning.

I am so blessed in that there were just so many people who assisted me in so many ways and I know that each one of them had been sent to me by our Father in Heaven. Without the help of these special people, it would have been very difficult to have made it outside of the home.

As I look back upon those six years which I spent in Green Acres, no matter how difficult they may have been or meaningless they may have felt, I thank God for each and every one of them. If I had not worked as a typist in the office, I would not have had the office experience that I now have. If I had not had so much to do with the people, both staff and residents of the home, I would not have acquired the ability to deal with different kinds of personalities and situations. If I had not continuously battled against a wall of rules and restrictions, I would not have appreciated the wonderful freedom that I now had. If I had not lived in the home, I would never have been strong enough, not only physically, but especially emotionally, to handle a job, let alone live in an environment where the only severely physically handicapped person was me! Whereas in a place like Green Acres, disability is part of everyday life, outside the shelter of the home, disability is something very out of the ordinary; I had the awesome task of looking past the hurtful comments and implications often made by many members of the public I served, and teaching everyone around me that disability does not mean no ability; that God does not make mistakes and that His power is truly made perfect in our weakness!

"And He has said to me, "My grace is sufficient for you, for power is perfected in weakness." Most gladly, therefore, I will rather boast about my weaknesses, so that the power of Christ may dwell in me."

— 2 Corinthians 12:9

As with our fish eagle, who is just so determined not to let that fish go, no matter how heavy it may be and no matter how much the weight of the fish drags it down, so must we persevere in whatever circumstances we may find ourselves, never letting go of the fact that we are never alone; we are surrounded by a great cloud of witnesses. In the eye of whatever storm we may find ourselves, may we, *"consider Him who has endured such hostility by sinners against Himself, so that you will not grow weary and lose heart."* Hebrews 12:3

Chapter Nine:
New Heights

"Is it at your command that the eagle mounts up and makes his nest on high? On the cliff he dwells and lodges, Upon the rocky crag, an inaccessible place. From there he spies out food; His eyes see it from afar."

— Job 39:27-29

The Push, a Story by David McNally

The eagle gently coaxed her offspring toward the edge of the nest. Her heart quivered with conflicting emotions as she felt their resistance to her persistent nudging. "Why does the thrill of soaring have to begin with the fear of falling?" she thought. This ageless question was still unanswered for her. As in the tradition of species, her nest was located high up on the shelf of a sheer rock face. Below there was nothing but air to support the wings of each chick. "Is it possible that this time it will not work?" she thought. Despite her fears, the eagle knew it was time. Her parental mission was all but complete. There remained one final task... THE PUSH.

The eagle drew courage from an innate wisdom. Until her children discovered their wings, there was no purpose for their lives. Until they learned how to soar, they would fail to understand the privilege it was to have been born an eagle. THE PUSH was the greatest gift she had to offer. It was her supreme act

113

of love. And so, one by one, she pushed them…And they flew.

THE PUSH; sometimes we need it, sometimes we need to give it!

A whole new world

Living on my own at the school just opened a whole new world of possibilities. Where, in Green Acres, it had been rather awkward for me to entertain visitors in my little room, I now had the privacy of a little living area in my flat. I was able to have visitors over anytime I wanted without having to worry about making sure that they did not come at times which were generally not standard visiting times, and then having to worry about them leaving in time before the main gate was locked at night. Setting a bad example by making tea for my visitors at times that were not standard tea times for everyone else was an issue at the home, but at the school, I didn't have to worry about all these factors. Visitors could come and go as they pleased and we didn't have to be concerned about overstepping the mark.

It took me a while to adjust to my newfound independence. In the beginning, whenever I would go out, I kept having to remind myself that I didn't have to tell anyone that I was going out or what time I would be back. Nor did I have to worry about being back by a certain time and perhaps be an inconvenience to the person giving me a lift home because he or she may have wanted to stay longer. As a result of no longer having a curfew, I was able to take part in so many more church activities as well as social ones. For a while, the highlight of my week was the Monday night prayer meeting, which sometimes did not end until the early hours of the next morning. Although I often felt the consequences the next day, they were by far outweighed by the blessings received from that awesome time of corporate prayer. This was a time where, by unison in prayer, we entered the very Throne Room of the Father, lay all our unrighteousness at His feet and upon rising from our knees, we were clothed with His righteousness, ready to face another week in His strength, and by His grace. It is my belief that such times of intimate prayer are times where one is closest to experiencing heaven on earth!

Soon after my move, I developed more very close friendships with various people in the church, particularly with the youth pastor, Glen, and his wife, Antje. These friendships resulted mainly from meeting together for weekly prayer and getting to know each other better through prayer. To me, it was amazing how God knew that I would need more friendships since I was living on my own, and how He provided them for me even before I felt the need for them.

A few months after moving into the flat and regularly attending prayer meetings, Glen asked if I would be interested in becoming involved with the youth ministry at the Church and eventually maybe becoming a youth leader. At first, I wondered if Glen was wearing blinkers. Couldn't he see I was disabled? Didn't he notice that I had a speech problem? How would the *teenagers* react to my Cerebral Palsy? By far, most importantly, did I really have the wisdom and maturity required to be a youth leader?

Despite all my concerns, I really wanted to work with the youth. Even before I had moved, my dream had been to be able to lead a Bible Study comprising of young girls. After much prayer, I started attending Friday night youth ministry meetings at the church. As a youth leader, you were required to lead an Accountability Discipleship (AD) group during the week, comprising of up to six or seven teenagers who attended Friday youth meetings. Many of the youth who came to this group were from the school and so it was not long after I had started attending youth that I started up my little AD group, consisting of two girls. Within a few weeks, it had grown to five girls. Was it all by chance that I happened to be living at the school? Did it just so happen that I was involved with the youth, with many students coming from the school and that I would be holding an AD group right there on the school premises, accessible for some of our youth to attend a weekly Bible study? Not at all! God is sovereign; He has a plan and purpose for everything and nothing ever happens by chance. About six weeks after becoming involved with the youth, I was officially welcomed as a youth leader. That evening, I shared my testimony with the youth and it was one time of sharing that I shall not easily forget. The Lord was really with me as He enabled me to speak so clearly; I was so encouraged by how the youth were listening so intently and the questions that were asked afterwards, even by a few of our usually restless youth, showed that much interest was taken in how God had worked in my life. Their response to me was such a contrast to what I had expected! I prayed that our youth would start to really grasp the fact that our God is so intimately involved with each and every one of their lives.

The joy of teaching

Being involved with the youth was such an honour for me. I found that there was such a difference between giving Bible study to intellectually impaired adults and teenage girls.

Where, with the former, it was often difficult to assess whether they had grasped the lesson due to a lack of interaction surrounding the lesson, with the young girls, they were just bursting with questions, and I had to lean so heavily on the Holy Spirit as I searched the Scriptures for answers. I loved this constant challenge as I learnt so much from having to search for answers. I know that I was far from being the perfect leader who had an answer to every question at her fingertips, or who had the ability to build perfect relationships with her teenagers and was able to counsel a teenager through any kind of crisis, but something that I did find to be so true during this time was that God does not need our abilities; He uses our availability! We all need to start somewhere and as we make ourselves available to His service, He guides us and teaches us along the way! As Jesus promises us in John 14:26: *"But the Helper, the Holy Spirit, whom the Father will send in My name, He will teach you all things, and bring to your remembrance all that I said to you."*

Being involved with the youth also played a role in helping me to overcome "self-consciousness", or more biblically, pride! No longer was I able to sit in the background, unnoticed. Much involvement and creativity was expected from each youth leader. It was no longer possible for me to maintain a low profile. I truly thank the Lord for using my involvement with the youth to help me grow in this area of my life. I have so much to share with people and yet, because I am so reserved and unwilling to make the first move, many people I meet on one-off occasions, leave none the wiser. They leave still feeling sorry for that poor spastic woman they met, the woman whose name is "Debbie". It is hard to approach people who don't know me; their reactions to me often hurt, but, as previously mentioned, these reactions are simply due to a lack of knowledge about disability. However, when I do make the first move, no matter how difficult it may be to step out of my little comfort zone and speak to people, aren't they encouraged as they reflect upon their own personal challenges? And —God is surely glorified when they realise that it's only my body that has been affected by the Cerebral Palsy and then hearing how God has just blessed me with such a happy, fulfilled life, despite my limitations.

Over the years of my stay at the school, I had many girls attend Bible study in my flat. As with any Bible study, I experienced great sadness as I watched some of the girls reject the Truth and follow after the pleasures of the world. However, I also experienced great joy as I watched many girls embrace the Truth, stand for it through their years of university and apply it in their adult lives.

Breaking free from Epanutin

I was thirty years old and it had been sixteen years since I had experienced my last convulsion; however, I was still on Epanutin, the medication used to control these convulsions, and I was still experiencing all the side effects of that medication. I began to wonder if continuing the medication and experiencing the painful mouth ulcers was worth it. I spoke to my good doctor about discontinuing the medication and although he agreed that I probably did not need it any longer because I was living on my own, he advised me not to try and come off it. The risk of having a convulsion alone in my flat was too high. In the past, as I had grown older, I would be able to feel when a convulsion was coming on and I would stop whatever I was doing and lie down. In the end, I would very rarely lose consciousness because I would fight it with everything I had. I reasoned with myself that this would still be possible. If I slowly weaned myself off the pills and if I did feel a possible convulsion coming on, I would put the kettle down, get out of the shower or stop whatever I was doing and lie down. I shared my desire only with my prayer partners, Glen, Antje and the rest of our small group and we prayed much about it. Two weeks later, I decided to take the chance and very slowly I began to wean myself off the medication. I started by reducing the dosage from one pill a day to one pill every second day for a month. Antje watched me closely, looking out for any tell-tale signs of the possibility of a convulsion. We continued to pray about it and the next month, I further reduced the dosage to one pill every third day for a month. Nobody was aware of the risk that I was taking, except the prayer group. So, I went on reducing the dosage until, after six months, I was down to one pill a week. I then confessed to my doctor, who was hardly surprised, being well aware of how stubborn I can be; he casually commented that one pill per week was useless and that I might as well discontinue the medication altogether! It has now been over ten years since I stopped the medication. Even though I have experienced times of intense stress over these ten years, the kind of stress which would have, in the past, triggered a multitude of convulsions, I have not experienced a convulsion since 1990, to God be the glory! I have enjoyed many years free from the side effects of the medication and it has been wonderful. The intensity of the mouth ulcers decreased drastically though I would still experience flare-ups when my immune system was very low.

(In writing this last paragraph, I have been very mindful of readers who may be or may know someone who is struggling with similar issues regarding medication for convulsions. In no way do I encourage anyone to follow in my footsteps and discontinue their medication. Each person has their own set of circumstances and one needs to very carefully evaluate their situation and seek the professional and medical advice and support of others before such drastic measures are taken).

Winds of change

Glen and Antje sadly left Polokwane in 2004, though I was privileged enough to visit them every year over the next five years. At first, Glen pastored a church down in Port Elizabeth, on the other side of the country. For three years I would save throughout the year for my air ticket and then I would fly down from Johannesburg to Port Elizabeth in December and visit them for ten days at a time. These visits were filled with so much laughter and many happy memories. I loved watching their two girls, Amanda and Rachel, grow over the years.

Even when Glen and Antje moved back up to Johannesburg at the end of 2007, my annual visits continued. I missed them terribly.

While Glen and Antje were still ministering in Polokwane, a young couple, Brendon and Belinda, began attending the young adult Bible study. Through our times of fellowship, we got to know each other well and by the time Glen and Antje left Polokwane, we had become very close friends. Brendon and Belinda lived and worked on a farm about 20km out of town and so they would often stay in town on a Sunday and have lunch with me so that they could attend the evening service without having to do two trips. We enjoyed many Sunday afternoons, sometimes engaging in serious conversation, and at other times, our afternoons were just filled with laughter. I would often spend weekends with them out on the farm and very special memories were born out of this friendship. I got to see prayers answered as little Rachel was blessed with a baby sister. Ruth was not just any baby sister; Belinda and Brendon had adopted her. I had a front-row seat as I watched in awe as each prayer was answered and how incredibly smoothly the adoption process had taken place.

I am always amazed by how the Lord has always blessed me with close friends in my life. Though the precious friends that move away never lose contact with me, I am always amazed by how God always ensures that I have very close friends with whom I can live life.

Back to the bush

It had always been my dream to spend a whole night in the great Kruger National Park, to lie and listen to the sounds of the wild bush again. I really missed Kariba. In my mind, the possibility of that dream ever coming true was very slim. I mentioned it once to Shirley, the friend who, together with her husband Gavin, would fetch me from my flat every Sunday for church. A few months later, in the middle of winter during the mid-year break, while at home on the farm enjoying the warmer climate, Shirley called. She invited me to join her and Gavin on a three-day trip to the Kruger Park. I was as excited as a little girl who had just heard that she was going on a trip to Disneyland! Those three days were filled with wonderful memories of very special sightings. I got to spend not just one night in the Park, but two. Both nights I was woken by the sound of hyena laughing in the distance and that was the ultimate highlight of my trip. As if things couldn't get any better, this was the first of many trips to the Kruger with Shirley.

Sadly, six months after our first trip, Gavin passed away from a brain aneurysm. The next couple of years were very difficult for Shirley, but, on occasion, the two of us would break away and go and spend a few days in the Kruger Park. Many wonderful and humorous memories were born out of these trips and over the years I have had the continued privilege of joining Shirley and her new husband, Seth, on these treasured trips.

It was on one of our trips, not long after Gavin had died, that Shirley noticed how incredibly weak I was becoming. I was too tired to even make the twenty-meter walk from the car to the ablutions. Shirley had to drive me there. This was very unusual for me and she wanted to get to the root of the problem. Shirley bombarded me with questions and came to the conclusion that I was not eating enough. I burn up so much more energy than an able-bodied person, not only because of energy consumed by continuous spasms but also because it takes so much more energy to live the independent lifestyle that I live, despite the severe Cerebral Palsy. Due to this, I need to eat more, and, more importantly, I needed to eat more of the right kind of food. At the time, I was not eating nearly as much as I needed to and I was becoming very weak. Though I got meals from the hostel kitchen, it was not always what I needed and I was often too tired in the evenings to make something for myself. Shirley took it upon herself to ensure that my freezer was always full of frozen cooked meals. She started by distributing plates to other ladies in the church and asking them, on the occasion when there was extra food on the table, to dish it up for me and freeze it. The ladies were more than willing to do this and at times, I had to ask them to slow down as I could not keep up and my freezer was not big enough to handle the amount of food. After a few weeks into this exercise, there was a remarkable improvement in my strength. For nine years, Shirley faithfully ensured that my freezer was always full of nutritious frozen food. What a pleasure it was for me to just take out a plate and pop it in the microwave oven, and within minutes, I have a hot ready-cooked meal!

Shirley, among many others, has been a wonderful friend to me over the many years she has known me and has become like a sister to me, having a tremendous impact on my life.

My little furry angel

After about eighteen months of living in my flat, I happened to mention to a colleague and close friend how nice it would be if I had a cat. However, I did not think this was possible as I still had my bird, Blondie, and everyone knows that a cat and a bird are not always a good combination, especially if the bird is out of his cage more often than not. Apart from that, because I went home four times a year during the school breaks, it would just not be practical to own a cat. Not long after the conversation, a friend of mine came into my office with a tiny feral kitten in her hands. She placed the bewildered-looking little thing into my lap and said, *"Don't say that I have never given you anything"*. She had found the little thing under her car. He had obviously crawled out from the bushes and had gotten lost. The children (being very superstitious of cats) had been trying to kill him. Despite my protests, she left the little kitten in my care.

After a few minutes in my lap, the kitten had made itself comfy and fallen asleep. I did not know what I was going to do: I definitely could not keep it. I organised some food for it and put it in a box; I had work to do and couldn't sit holding a sleeping kitten for the rest of the day! The kitten wanted to know nothing about the box and I had to somehow carry on working with this tiny thing in my lap. That day, after work, I organised a sandbox for it in my flat and found a lift into town. I just wanted to get a deworming tablet and some kitten food, just enough to last until I found a home for it. Upon returning from town, not sure what state I would find my flat in, I walked in to find that the little thing had conveniently made his way up onto my bed and was curled up in a neat little ball, fast asleep. I had to do something fast because this little thing was crawling its way into my heart. During the course of that evening, I was already considering the possibilities of actually keeping the kitten. Being very stripy, I named him "Tigger", and for eight years, Tigger was the source of much joy in my life. Much to my surprise, Tigger adapted very well to my lifestyle. He went out at night when it was quiet to do his business, so I had no need for a smelly sandbox in my flat. Tigger came home to my parents with Blondie and me during the school holidays and had a pen (especially built by my dad) where he could do his business protected from the dogs. Often, much to my disgust, Tigger would proudly bring in headless mice which he had caught during the night. Thankfully, he was well aware of the fact that Blondie was not on the menu. It was not unusual to have Blondie sitting on my shoulder and Tigger on my lap. Tigger was truly a gift from God. Sensing very quickly when I was down, he would come and snuggle up as close to me as he could, very rarely leaving me.

Tigger has also played an active role in my AD group. Many of my girls were terribly afraid of cats, but Tigger, being "Mr Affectionate" himself, would make his way around the room, rubbing himself against legs or jumping up onto laps. It could be quite unnerving when, during a time of prayer, one of the girls would suddenly let out a screech as Tigger brushed past. It was never very long before a newcomer got used to Tigger and learnt that there was no truth to all the superstitions they had about cats. Tigger had suffered from kidney stones since he was two years old, but with special food from the vet each month, I was able to manage his condition very well. He had developed terrible abscesses from fighting with wild cats and had to undergo major surgery to remove these abscesses. All these visits to the vet were very costly, but my Tigger was so worth every penny. Sadly, in 2011, Tigger became very ill. I could see that he was not himself, and, as each day went by, he became more and more lethargic. My wonderful friend Liz took Tigger to the vet one morning for me on her way to work, giving the vet strict instructions not to call and inform me of Tigger's condition. Liz, being a doctor, had her suspicions of what was wrong with Tigger and if she was correct, she wanted to be the one to tell me.

That afternoon, I eagerly waited for her to return Tigger to me. When she eventually arrived with Tigger, one look at her face told me everything. Tigger had Feline Leukaemia and the vet had given him six weeks to live. I was devastated!

The next day, he was ten times worse than what he had been just the day before; I was amazed at how fast Tigger's condition had deteriorated. I made the awful decision to have him put to sleep, as I couldn't stand to watch him suffer.

Once again, I was surrounded by the comfort of my precious friends. Martin was a store consultant and after assisting me one day in the store, he took it upon himself to be a friend to me. That afternoon, Liz, Martin and I took Tigger and had him put down. We all sobbed, including the poor vet, but I knew that I had done the right thing.

Independent living

Living independently does not come without its challenges. Although I enjoyed the loyalty and faithfulness of Rahab's help, there were always times when I was alone in my little haven. It was during these times that I found myself constantly calling out to the Father for help. I needed Him to not only help me guard my ever wandering thoughts, but more practically, I needed Him to help me get up and ready in time for work in the mornings; I needed Him to help me successfully get through each day at work, with a smile on my face despite intense muscular pain, or harsh treatment often encountered by customers. I needed Him to assist me as I removed a jug of milk from the fridge and poured boiling water as I made myself a warm beverage such as coffee, hot chocolate or soup. I needed Him to get me safely in and out of the shower every day and for over nine years, not once did I not experience His loving hand over me. With each passing day, I was more amazed at how He was constantly there for me, despite my many sinful ways. Yes, let us not for one moment forget that although I have many limitations, I am just as capable of committing the same kind of sins as anybody else and I praise Him with all my heart that His mercies are new every morning.

> *"The LORD'S loving kindnesses indeed never cease, For His compassions never fail. They are new every morning; Great is Your faithfulness."*

> — **Lamentations 3:22-23**

Sometimes in our desperation, we are unable to see the hand of God in the midst of our circumstances. At times, when it feels as if we are just living a life of existence without any purpose, it is so hard to see how God could be using this "meaningless" time in our lives for His glory and our good.

When young Joseph was sold by his brothers as a slave to the Egyptians, as he was torn away from his beloved father, as he had to learn and adapt to the strange Egyptian lifestyle, I am certain that he never imagined that in time he would become second to Pharaoh and that God would use his situation in such a way that he would be instrumental in saving the small group of Israelites from dying of starvation. I am sure that he never dreamed that as a result of his slavery, a small group of Israelites would multiply in the land of Egypt and become a great nation, Genesis 37-50.

Like Joseph, I can stand tall because I know that *"for in Him we live and move and exist,"* Acts 17:28

May we never forget:

> *"And we know that God causes all things to work together for good to those who love God, to those who are called according to His purpose."*

> **— Romans 8:28**

Chapter Ten:
Breaking Through the Clouds

"...I carried you on eagles' wings and brought you to Myself."

— Exodus 19:4

Awakening before dawn, the eagle begins its serenade, a song well-known across Africa. About 40 minutes before sunrise, the air throughout the sub-Sahara fills with the chorus of singing pairs. The calls serve as a territorial signal. The "tune" may be produced in flight while the eagle searches for potential prey.

Another change in current

During this time, Liz, a doctor studying ophthalmology, became very much more part of my circle of friendship. Liz comes from Johannesburg and has an incredibly caring and outgoing personality. Around this time, Brendon and Belinda began talking about moving to New Zealand. Selfishly, I consoled myself with the thought that the immigration process would take ages and then there was even the chance that their visas would be denied. Before I knew it, Brendon had obtained a job in New Zealand and shortly after, late in 2007, we were saying our heart-wrenching goodbyes. However, I was really happy for them as the four of them quickly settled down so well in their new country.

I was thankful for the friendship that I had with Liz. We regularly went out on Friday nights for dinner and a movie. Liz worked long, hard hours at the hospital, so these social evenings were not only so good for me but they gave Liz a nice distraction from the pressure of her job.

Life experience

The year 2007 was a year that would change my life! An experience that is feared by most women became a reality in my life, throwing me into excruciating turmoil, the repercussions of which lasted for 8 years. The details of this experience could be elaborated on in future writings but suffice to say that the Lord is faithful, He loves those whom He calls His own and no matter how dark the circumstance in which we may find ourselves, He is always right there with us. *"Never will I leave you; never will I forsake you."* Hebrew 13:5. His promises are true, His love is real.

I was especially thankful that by this time my friendship with Liz had deepened and during this time she became a great help and counsellor to me through the months and years that followed.

Though a very difficult time, I am thankful for the lessons I learnt as He faithfully carried me through. Once again, the promise of Romans 8:28 rang so true and I experienced great spiritual growth.

Strike number two

According to the superstitious, if a young lady is asked to be a bridesmaid three times, she will never get married. Thankfully, I do not hold to that belief and I am also completely content as a single lady.

Cristo had experienced his fair share of disappointments in the dating game,   but in late 2008, after having his heart broken, he became good friends with a wonderful lady. Lee is older than Cristo and having experienced great heartbreak herself, she was able to come alongside Cristo and help him through his heartache.

For a change, this was one of Cristo's girlfriends with whom I could enjoy a good relationship. She accepted and treated me no differently and loved me for who I am.

Cristo and Lee fell in love and decided to get married in March of 2010.

Lee was adamant that I should be one of her bridesmaids, but according to my mind, she hardly knew me. Once again, I was plagued by those same concerns that had worried me with Irmela's wedding. At one point, Lee actually took it personally and became offended that I "didn't want" to be her bridesmaid. Sadly, this is what it took for me to finally see that her request had solely been out of a genuine desire for me to play such an important part in her wedding and not out of sympathy or pity. What a tremendous privilege it was, especially as it was my brother's wedding. Though, once again, I could not play the true role of a bridesmaid, I had the wonderful privilege of praying with Lee on the morning of her wedding.

Lee and I are extremely close and I truly am blessed to have her as my sister-in-law. I shudder as I reflect upon Cristo's former girlfriends and imagine how differently things could have turned out.

Pressure building

The school was continuously expanding and more children were being enrolled. The school was growing and so was my workload. I didn't want to admit it, but I was starting to take the strain.

Keeping effective control of stock and seeing to the needs of customers and staff remained a priority to the further detriment of my health.

Over time, my health became very poor. It became the norm for me to get bronchitis at least four times a year and to be on at least five courses of antibiotics during the winter. This resulted in me having to take sick leave for weeks at a time. So often, the fear of losing my job because of being sick caused me much stress, further weakening my immune system, and, in 2010, I landed up in hospital with pneumonia.

Like so many times before, Bev stepped in and took care of my every need while I was in hospital and upon discharge, I stayed with Bev and her husband Chris for ten days to ensure complete recovery.

In 2011 after Tigger died, I began living with Liz. At first, it was only going to be temporary as she was studying for a major exam and I wanted to be there to support her. Liz was house-sitting a four-bedroom house for friends, Matt and Elizabeth, a physiotherapist couple. Matt and Elizabeth had recently purchased the house with the intention of turning it into a practice in the near future. There was no shortage of space.

Liz would drop me off at work in the mornings and pick me up on her way home in the evenings.

We got on so well. It really was wonderful to be around such great company. We worked hard towards Liz's exams and she did everything she could to make life easier for me, despite my protests. She would insist that by doing things that took so much of my energy to do myself, she was easing my physical stress and she was right! Simple things like helping me to get dressed after a hot bath in winter, blow-drying my hair and so much more, made the world of difference. As a doctor, she knew that my muscles would go into worse spasms the longer I was exposed to the cold, and the harder I tried to get dressed quickly, the more energy I would use.

Through our physiotherapist friends, Liz took a dry needling course, especially so that she could perform the procedure on me. Dry needling is the process in which special needles are inserted into a muscular knot enabling blood and oxygen to flow through the knot, which causes the muscle to release.

Due to the intensity of my job at the school, the responsibility of so much money and the stress of ensuring stock control accuracy, I would come home with some seriously impressive muscle knots. Needless to say, I would often look like a pin cushion after Liz was finished with me! The relief that followed far outweighed the discomfort of having each needle inserted into each knot.

What was supposed to be only two months, until Liz had written her exams, ended up being an entire year. What an incredible year that was, each day filled with so much laughter! She is as stubborn as I, if not more so. At times, when I showed signs of the beginnings of a cold, she would simply refuse to take me to work. No matter how much I would protest, she would not be persuaded otherwise and she would ensure that Sonja was informed of my absence. As usual, I would worry about missing work. I felt that I was not "sick enough" to stay away from work, but Liz was right; treating a cold in its early stages would prevent the onset of bronchitis.

Since my job at the school was a half-day job, around 2010, I worked for Peter, an insurance broker in town, for over a year doing general administration two afternoons every week. I had met Peter through his wife, Jackie, who was one of the teachers at school and she had spoken highly of my administrative skills. Peter had decided to give me a chance to earn a little extra money by helping out in the office during the afternoons. I enjoyed being exposed to different things and because work at the school was becoming all the more strenuous, I had to be on the lookout for alternative employment possibilities.

Rib record

In the early hours one morning, I got out of bed to use the bathroom. Still half asleep, I was especially unsteady, and, as I lowered myself onto the toilet, I fell sideways hitting the side of the bath. The handrail of the bath went into my ribs, breaking two of them. I was very aware of the breaks as wearing various clothing items, coughing or even laughing was extremely painful. God's loving kindness was evident even in this because I was not alone when I had this fall, as Liz had been asleep in the room next door.

I became ill with the flu a few weeks after the fall. Liz was worried that because I was unable to cough properly due to the pain from the broken ribs, I would be more susceptible to pneumonia, so once again, I spent another week in bed. Sonja was becoming impatient as it was during the time of year when budgets for the next year's stock needed to be submitted and I was not at work to complete their compilation. The tension was mounting!

Things came to a head when, after a series of false accusations, I experienced another bad fall in my office and broke another two ribs as I fell onto the arm of my office chair. After a heavy day at work, poor Liz still insisted on taking me to the hospital that evening for X-rays. She wanted to ensure the breaks were not of such a nature that they could cause damage to my lungs. Upon studying my chest X-rays the next day with our physiotherapist friends, Matt, Elizabeth and Liz found them to be a very interesting topic of discussion, especially when Elizabeth spotted an old break that had healed years ago. The total of broken ribs was now five, one of which I had never even been aware of. Two years later, I would have another fall breaking four more ribs!

I am sure that if I had X-rays now, we would see an impressive record of at least ten breaks.

Season of change

Chatting over dinner one evening after a very tiring day at work, Liz confirmed once again what I already knew: it was time for me to move on. I was heading for my tenth year at the school and torrents of water had gushed under the bridge. The school had changed and I could not follow its course, my health would not allow me to keep up with its pace.

I resigned at the end of October 2011 and the mission team from church descended upon the school with trucks, bakkies and mini-buses. With one swoop, they had packed and loaded up the contents of my entire flat, including my little garage which had been put up for my electric wheelchair; with one scoop, they moved everything I had into the house where I was staying with

Liz.

A new position

I accepted a permanent position with Peter, the insurance broker, as his Personal Assistant and started on Monday the 1st of November 2011. This job was also a half-day job and my salary was double what I had received at the school. I had not realised how incredibly intense a PA's job would be, but I was up for the challenge. Since I could not take notes in morning meetings, I suggested to Peter that we get a Dictaphone, which we did, and it helped immensely, especially in those "he said/she said" situations. My job entailed much telephonic communication which was simply impossible for me with my speech impediment. Although the ladies in the office who were dealing with insurance claims kindly said they would be happy to make all my calls for me, many of these calls would take up so much of their time. For example, I would be requested to acquire personal information from bank accounts on Peter's behalf. Naturally, bankers would have to verify the validity of the person requesting the information. The fact that the caller was calling on behalf of Peter's PA who had been requested to obtain the information only complicated things a hundredfold.

I had to ensure that accounts were paid and up to date. This entailed writing out cheques – and of course, barely being able to write, this too was impossible. Once again, I had to rely on the other ladies in the office. Part of my duties required me to run errands outside of the office. This too was not possible, as driving a vehicle was required.

I wondered how long the office ladies would put up with my endless requests for assistance which kept them away from their own work.

The office was on the second floor of a shopping arcade, so, in order to get to work, I had to climb two flights of stairs every morning and back down them every afternoon. Being so determined and stubborn, I didn't see the stairs as a problem. They were an inconvenience but I was not going to let them deter me from making a success of my new job. I felt that I had to make this work; *Who else would employ me?* I thought. Once again, Liz knew better. She was concerned that I was tiring myself out, and, for the period of a month, we tried to find alternate ways for me to get up to the office without climbing the stairs! The arcade did not have lifts, only very steep slopes, too steep for Liz to push me up in the wheelchair. We would ask the car guards for their help but this was not part of their job description and so they were not prepared to assist. After exploring different options of trying to eliminate the stairs, we had to resign ourselves to the fact that I had no choice but to use the stairs.

Another concern for Liz was that the stairs, being on the exterior of the building, would not be ideal for me in the winter, especially as I started work at 07:00 and it took me at least ten minutes to climb them. Being exposed to the cold for long periods of time along with the physical exertion of climbing the stairs would put me at greater risk of getting bronchitis or pneumonia.

The family grows

One evening, I accompanied Liz to the hospital out in the rural area where she worked, as I often did. These trips were often filled with much chatter and laughter. On this particular trip out, she wanted to introduce me to an abandoned puppy that she had befriended and was sharing her lunch with. Due to the harsh way this puppy had been treated, it was very wary and skittish towards any human being. Liz called the dog 'Charlotte' but upon closer examination, 'Charlotte' became 'Charlie'. I fell in love with Charlie as soon as I saw him. He was so skinny and neglected, but in his eyes, one could see such a gentle, loving nature.

Liz and I spent an entire hour luring Charlie into the back seat of the car. We even used frozen food which I had brought home for dinner to entice him and finally, after much love and patience, we got him into the car - realising only after that we hadn't exactly bargained on having a dog. We wondered what our landlords would think. I called Elizabeth on our way home with Charlie, hoping they wouldn't have a problem with Charlie on their property. Being as sharp as Elizabeth is, she burst out laughing. Interrupting me, she had guessed we had Charlie in the car and commented that she had known that it was just a matter of time. Elizabeth, an animal lover herself, was excited about Charlie as her two puppies would soon enjoy play dates with Charlie and later the three dogs would become inseparable.

Charlie took time to settle down. At first, Charlie would easily startle; he was very skittish. For the first few days, he would not dare to come into the house. Everyone had chased him whenever he ventured too near the hospital, so for him, crossing the threshold of the doorway into the house was a daunting experience. However, after a week, Charlie had become a third member of the household. He settled down very well and became an incredibly affectionate dog, bringing much more laughter into the house. Due to his past, Charlie became very protective over Liz and me. Regardless of skin colour, if Charlie did not approve of anyone, they did not dare enter the house without the assurance that Charlie was locked up.

A few months after getting Charlie, I felt ready to get another kitten. I missed having a furry ball cuddle up to me at night. My mum found kittens advertised in the paper during one of my visits to the farm, and, on our way back to Polokwane, we stopped and I chose the cutest of the litter, the one with the longest hair of course. I named her Phoebe.

Phoebe was a beautiful cat. She was grey and white and had the longest of eyelashes.

Liz and I, not to mention Elizabeth, were thrilled to have a kitten in the house. Phoebe settled down quickly and she became the best of friends with Charlie; they would often curl up, sleeping together in Charlie's bucket. When Elizabeth brought her puppies over to play with Charlie, little Phoebe was never intimidated by their boisterous play and often stood her ground.

Phoebe and I became extremely close. Each afternoon when I returned from work, she would meet me at the gate and walk with me into the house, leading me straight to the cupboard in which she knew her treats were kept.

Never-ending journey

I was very privileged to be invited to spend a week away with Liz and her family in Mborne, a beautiful place that her parents had bought in the 1980s down in the Natal Midlands.

Liz's dad had kindly called us the morning we left and informed us of the hectic Easter traffic through Johannesburg, where tollgates were backed up for 20km. He had advised us to take another very scenic route, through the province of Mpumalanga.

We had left that morning at six, expecting the journey to take us only nine hours! The journey was going well until around four in the afternoon when we came across an incredibly long traffic jam and we sat in the jam for well over an hour! The cause of the jam turned out to be road works! This is when our journey no longer went as smoothly. Not only did it seem as if there were road works around every corner but we kept getting caught up in traffic jams. To make matters worse, as darkness fell, we began getting lost over and over again. The road was unfamiliar to us and the road works just made things more confusing. South Africa was hosting the 2010 Soccer World Cup and so roads were being maintained or widened in preparation for this big event. The fact that fatigue was setting in only made the journey more difficult!

Eventually, we stopped at a service station where Liz put her head back and slept for a couple of hours and we were back on the road again, either getting lost every now and then or patiently waiting at countless points of road works!

In order to ensure that poor Liz did not fall asleep at the wheel, with my 'angelic' voice, I sang to her the song that I knew she most despised and it worked; Liz's trying to keep me quiet kept her awake.

Towards what we thought was the end of our journey at 02:00 the next morning, we found ourselves lost again, this time on a quiet, single-lane road.

Here, much to our horror, we hit a pothole and got a puncture. It was pitch dark, there were no street lights and, in the distance, we could hear the sound of hunting dogs. This was a time that we really did not want to see the headlights of another car, especially at 2 o'clock in the morning. Poor Liz insisted that I remain in the car for safety reasons and so that I could try to keep watch while she changed the wheel. Liz did a brilliant job of changing the wheel though just as she was tightening the last bolt, the car battery died. We had kept the car running for light, which in turn, had killed the car's battery. We had no idea of where we were, so calling Liz's family would not have helped; it would only have made them anxious. Two single ladies broken down on an unfamiliar road in the early hours of the morning was a scary experience. But God...! Without realizing it, when the wheel punctured, by God's grace, the car had come to a halt at the top of a hill and we were able to freewheel down the hill and get the car started! Many prayers of thanks went up to our precious heavenly Father after that!

We found our way back onto the highway. After more driving around, much to our relief, Liz found the route with which she was familiar and we finally reached our destination at 05:00 am, just in time to see the sun rising.

The heavens declare the glory of God; the skies proclaim the work of his hands. Day after day they pour forth speech; night after night they display knowledge. There is no speech or language where their voice is not heard. Their voice goes out into all the earth, their words to the ends of the world. In the heavens he has pitched a tent for the sun, which is like a bridegroom coming forth from his pavilion, like a champion rejoicing to run his course. It rises at one end of the heavens and makes its circuit to the other; nothing is hidden from its heat. Psalm 19:1-6

The 23-hour journey was truly an adventure but we really thank the Lord for His amazing protection! Needless to say, I slept the whole first day of our holiday and this was just the beginning of an incredibly restful week.

A day like no other

On the 1st of December 2011, I went about my morning as I had done for the entire first month of working for Peter. Liz had dropped me off at work, I climbed the stairs, attended the morning meeting, but as I exited Peter's office, I noticed that I was short of breath. As the minutes passed, I felt my breathing becoming more difficult. I thought twice about notifying Liz, not wanting to alarm her over "nothing". However, thankfully I finally did call her. I had chest pain, was very out of breath and I had a very rapid heartbeat. Upon telling her my symptoms and hearing how out of breath I was over the phone, Liz immediately called Bev and asked her to take me to the doctor. Liz (being at work in a rural hospital 40km away) called me consistently every five minutes to monitor my breathing until Bev and I reached the doctor. My doctor sent me for X-rays and what both Liz and my good doctor had suspected was confirmed: I had a pneumothorax, or collapsed lung, which is the collection of air in the space around the lungs. This build-up of air puts pressure on the lung, so it cannot expand as much as it normally does when you take a breath, and in severe cases, it can be fatal. We are not sure what caused it, although we suspect that it was a combination of the cracked ribs and the strenuous exercise of climbing the stairs.

By around 11am that morning, I found myself booked into hospital and lying in the casualty ward, with Liz at my side assuring me, while another doctor inserted a chest drain between my ribs to drain the air that was accumulating around my lung. This procedure was one of the most painful I have yet experienced. My drain was removed after three days. Though I returned to work two weeks later, it took me at least six weeks to fully recover.

Tides of change

I spent Christmas 2011 at home with my family. It was a lovely Christmas with the whole family together. I enjoyed it especially as I did not have the craziness of the "back to school" beginning of the year rush on my mind. However, in the back of my mind, I knew that big changes would come with 2012. Liz, being extremely unhappy where she worked, had gone for a job interview and I knew that if she got the job, she would relocate and be with her family in Johannesburg, three and a half hours from Polokwane. The war that raged in my mind almost made me ill. I so wanted Liz to be happy, but that would mean that our little comfort zone at home would be shattered. Needless to say, Liz did get the job in Johannesburg and she was due to start on the first of March 2012. I was grateful for the couple of months we had left together.

Upon returning from the Christmas holidays, reality began to set in; Liz was really moving to Johannesburg! Questions raised in my mind were: *How would I get to and from work? Would I cope living alone in this 4-bedroom house? How long would I be able to stay in this house before Matt & Elizabeth would need to begin renovating the house?* I was sad that Charlie was going. I consoled myself with the thought that at least I would still have Phoebe.

Liz and I spent a weekend in Johannesburg late that January. I wanted to see where she would be working and while we were there, we looked at potential residential areas closest to her place of work.

As Liz wheeled me through the hospital where she would soon be working, a heavy feeling came over me and as the tour finished, I was very close to tears. The hospital was so dilapidated, the corridors were damp and dark, doors creaked and I kept hoping that she would change her mind, but this move would be the only way that Liz could further her studies and was the next step up towards her realizing her dream of becoming a specialist in the field of ophthalmology. I consoled myself with the thought that this hospital would soon be receiving an angel in the form of a human - *"Liz would brighten this dull place up"*. I was determined to enjoy the weeks we had left together before Liz moved.

Valentine's Day!

As single ladies, Liz and I were never too excited about Valentine's Day but the 14th of February 2012 would be a Valentine's Day of note. I awoke that morning concerned that I hadn't seen Phoebe since the early evening before: she hadn't been on my bed the entire night. We had looked for her before we had gone to bed; not finding her, we had concluded that she was outside somewhere in the garden, playing. Morning had come and she was still nowhere to be seen. We quickly got ready for work, had breakfast and got into the car to start searching for her.   As we came around one of the corners, close to the house, we saw her lifeless body on the road; she had been hit by a car.

We were both shocked and devastated. We could not understand why this should happen "now". The timing was just so wrong. We both took the day off work; we were just too upset and flabbergasted. Liz was due to leave in two weeks' time with Charlie. Phoebe was gone; in two weeks, would I be completely alone?

During that day, Liz and I spent the day together chatting about what possibilities the future could hold over countless mugs of tea and coffee. At one stage, Liz calmly commented that she thought that I should resign from my job as Personal Assistant to Peter. At first, I thought she was kidding, but she wasn't - she was dead serious! She felt that the job was far too strenuous for me. I was stunned! It was as if Liz had just set fire to a beehive! "So, you are suggesting that despite you leaving, I should quit my job as well?" I asked. *Finding another job would be very difficult and what about the employer getting to know me and my capabilities, what about all the logistics of settling down, finding transport to and from a new job? Where would I find another job anyway?* Resigning from my job was a very daunting thought, and initially, I would not even entertain the idea. Liz's next comment was that I didn't have to find another job! I burst out laughing. I was now sure that she was kidding. Liz was not kidding and as she explained her "absurd" suggestion, I began to see her reasoning behind it.

Resigning and staying at home would take an incredible amount of stress off me. For a start, I would not have to constantly worry about finding lifts to and from work; I would not have to face flights of stairs each day, especially during winter; and above all, I would not have the stress of trying to cope in a job that was simply not at all possible for me to execute. I knew that Peter was not getting the standard of work that he expected and that it was frustrating him.

So, my next concern was finance; though I was blessed to have a regular source of income besides my salary in the form of a Disability Pension, it would not be enough to cover my insurances, hospital plan and still feed myself. Liz assured me that this was a minor concern and that she had already taken it into consideration.

After thrashing out the pros and cons of resigning, by the end of what was a very sad day, I climbed into bed feeling ten tons lighter, as I had decided that it was in the best interests of all concerned that I should resign from my job. I had not realized just how much pressure I had been putting upon myself by trying to force what was not possible. I finally acknowledged what I had known deep down inside since the first day that I started my job as Personal Assistant: I simply could not cope!

The next day, I handed in my resignation and gave two weeks' notice. Not only did I not have a job, but I would be occupying a mansion on my own. Everything felt surreal. I wondered what the future held! My friend of many years, Shirley, consoled me by commenting on how she could not wait to see what plans the Lord next had in store for my life. At the time, her remark felt a little callous, but I knew from where it was coming. Shirley was reminding me that our Lord truly loves His children and that He will never leave His children nor forsake them. I had to know and trust that despite how everything felt, looked and seemed, my God still had plans for my life.

Over the weeks leading up to Liz's departure, Liz came up with so many plans that would enable me to continue enjoying simple pleasures to which I had become accustomed while living with her. For example, I loved my bath.

At the school, my little shower had been so temperamental; climbing into a wonderful hot bath was an absolute treat, but I needed assistance getting in and out of the bath. The bathroom in the main bedroom of the house had a wonderfully low bath which made it easy for me to get in and out of it on my own, but it was still too dangerous for me to do so without anyone around, as the risk of slipping and falling was too great. Liz came up with the idea of installing a heavy-duty rail which I could hold on to while getting in and out of the bath. She went to a great deal of trouble and expense of finding just the right rail and with Matt's help, kindly installed it for me.

Liz even gave her washing machine to me as a gift; there is simply no end to this lady's kindness.

The time came for Liz to leave. I caught a ride with her through to Johannesburg and spent a couple of weeks with my dear friends, Glen and Antje.

My visit with them during this time of change and uncertainty did me the world of good. By now, their family of four had grown and I was privileged enough to meet newly adopted little Eden. As usual, we enjoyed not only times of great laughter but also times of deep discussion and prayer which would often take us into the early hours of the morning. My time with them was truly refreshing and exactly what I needed to prepare me for the months that lay ahead. During the two weeks that I was away, Liz had returned to Polokwane to collect more of her belongings. Walking into the house upon my return was an eerie, heart-wrenching experience. Although some of Liz's furniture was still in the house, the house had such a lonely echo ring to it.

> *The LORD will keep you from all harm-- he will watch over your life;*
>
> — Psalm 121:7

Chapter Eleven:
Soaring above the Clouds

"Praise the Lord, my soul; all my inmost being, praise his holy name!... who satisfies your desires with good things so that your youth is renewed like the eagle's."

— **Psalm 103:1 & 5**

When perched and singing, the eagle theatrically throws its head back and belts out its song. The African fish eagle sings this loud, cheerful song throughout the day, often in female-initiated duets. A pair will normally remain together after the breeding season.

Gratitude changes attitude

In the weeks to come, with the help of the domestic worker (kindly paid for by Liz) who came once a week to clean the house, I took out my own furniture which had been stored in one of the rooms and managed to make the house (or at least the lounge) feel a bit more homely again. It was time to lift my head and make the most of my situation. I had so much to be thankful for. I no longer had to wake up at the crack of dawn to get ready for work every day. Winter was just around the corner and I was able to stay indoors and keep warm. Matt had very kindly set up a Wi-Fi connection in the house for me to use as much as I wanted.

Although my time was my own, I was determined not to waste it. I was up and dressed every morning by 7:30, I had my breakfast and then sat at the computer for most of the day. I tried to teach myself how to design websites, but soon realised that I did not have the perseverance or patience to sit and learn the coding used in website designing. However, I spent many hours on Skype with friends from all over the world. Speaking to my very close friends in New Zealand, Brendon and Belinda, almost became a daily privilege. It was great to be such a part of their daily lives even though they are halfway around the world. I would even take part in their Thursday evening Bible studies which were late Thursday morning, South African time.

Though my thoughts were prone to wander into dangerous territory at times, between Brendon and Belinda, Antje and Glen, as well as many other precious brothers and sisters from the church, I was held accountable continuously with regard to living my life to the honour of my Lord, regardless of the fact that I was mostly on my own.

There was a shopping centre not far from the house and I was able to go down in my motorised wheelchair and do my own shopping. Nonetheless, a roster had been drawn up by the elders of the church and a different lady from the church had made herself available to me for each day of the week in order to help me with transport if it was required.

My faithful Rahab would catch a taxi once a week on a Tuesday evening from the school to where I was staying and would spend the night with me in the house. She was very concerned about me staying alone and I was grateful for her company.

Though I was alone for most of the time, I always felt His presence with me. I stayed on my own in the house for three months without incident, no serious falls, I experienced no criminal activity and I never went to bed hungry. In fact, as I look back, I see that time as a time of great rest and refreshment, a gift from the Lord.

Each week when I attended the Wednesday evening Bible study, Pastor

Steve would encourage me by informing me that the elders of the church were working on a solution to my situation as everyone was aware of the fact that I could not stay in the house indefinitely. The idea of going back to Green Acres made my stomach churn. However, I knew that if it was in God's plan for me to go back there, He would enable me to make peace with it and to accept that even this would be part of His plan for me.

Renewed Health

It was during this time that Belinda and Brendon introduced me to a direct selling company. Mannatech owns over 100 patents on a groundbreaking technology. Belinda's main reason for introducing me to the technology was to help build and support my immune system. Over the last few years, I had become so run down and the state of my health was a real concern to those close to me. Belinda and Brendon, true to who they are, had done in-depth research on Mannatech as well as the technology which this company represented before introducing it to me. They had been impressed to learn what this technology had done for so many people with various health challenges. They were impressed by the values that the company stood for. Belinda and Brendon very kindly sponsored my starter pack and were excited to see how my health would benefit. From the time that I started using this technology, my health has improved wonderfully. The first thing that I noticed was that I no longer experienced such severe flare-ups of mouth ulcers. Instead of lasting for weeks on end, my migraines now only last a couple of days. Though still wearing glasses, my eyesight also improved to such an extent that I began seeing beautiful detail on birds sitting up in treetops, where, in the past, I was lucky if I could barely make out the shape of the bird, let alone appreciate its beautiful detail.

After three years of being on this technology, for the very first time, I found that I could use my right hand to pick up a very small sweet and put it into my mouth. Up until then, my right hand had been scrunched up in a tight fist. I have since found myself using my right hand more frequently.

In the six years that I have been on Mannatech technology, I have only twice required a course of antibiotics. My health and general wellbeing have truly improved in leaps and bounds. Belinda, Brendon and I began exploring the business side of the company and since then I have had the joy of introducing this technology to others.

By God's grace, I worked my way up a few leadership levels in this network marketing company. This gave me a wonderful platform outside of the church where I was able to encourage and inspire people from all walks of life. I was able to share my life with thousands of other people. I praise God for this wonderful opportunity.

A New Beginning

About six weeks after Liz had left Polokwane, Ian, one of our church elders, came to see me. Ian said that the elders had decided to let me help out in the office part-time. He also shared with me that, after much discussion, the elders had decided to renovate a portion of the old seminary hostel into a little flat for me. The front portion of the old hostel was still being used as a dining hall and kitchen for the seminary students, but the back portion, which consisted of two bedrooms and a bathroom, would be turned into my living area; I was speechless! As if that wasn't enough, Ian asked what special adaptations should be taken into consideration during the renovations. He told me that the men's Bible study had already poured concrete and built wheelchair-friendly slopes not only leading into the hostel but, much to my amazement, over the entire church property. Wherever it was not wheelchair accessible, a slope had been built. Not only was I going to live on the church grounds, but I would be helping out at the church office. I was truly overwhelmed. How perfect! I would be living and working on the church property. Transport to and from the office would no longer be an issue and neither would transport to and from church on Sundays; this in itself was such an incredible blessing. I would be helping out in an environment closest to my heart, though at that time I was not sure what kind of assistance I would be offering.

My meals would be provided for me out of the seminary hostel kitchen. The cleaning of my flat would be done by the ladies who worked for the hostel.

Shirley came with me when Ian took me to show me the room which they were planning to renovate. It was a large room with a bathroom en-suite. The bathroom had an unusually large shower, large enough for me to have a chair put in to use when necessary. I noted that my bathroom had a door; how wonderful for when I have visitors, as my bathroom at the school only had a curtain separating it from the rest of the open-plan flat.

The room had sliding doors leading out into the back garden which was filled with bushes and shrubs.

Much to my joy, Shirley and Ian decided that I would also need the room next door which could be turned into a little kitchen. A doorway would be broken through from the main room into the second room, giving me easy access to the second room. The second room had built-in cupboards which would prove to be invaluable. The rooms would be fixed up and painted out. There are no words to describe the joy and excitement I felt that day.

The church went to great expense to ensure that my new home was perfect. I was even blessed with a steel kitchen sink unit. With savings, I purchased a beautiful pine kitchen unit with drawers.

I had a lovely small set of four chairs and a table that would fit beautifully in the kitchen. There would even be space for my washing machine and tumble dryer.

The day finally came for me to move. Bev had been coming over all week to help me pack! Once again, so many people from the church showed up at the house with their trucks and trailers to assist with the move. All, including me, were once again horrified to see how much stuff I owned! We all wondered if everything would fit into my new home. Amazingly, in the end, after a day of very hard work, a place for all my furniture had been found. The men had fit everything in beautifully and the place didn't even look crammed. Much to my joy, the ladies had spent the day in my kitchen, unpacking boxes and arranging my little kitchen. All this help was priceless to me. By the end of that day, only a few boxes containing mainly pictures and books remained unpacked. I was in awe that evening as I sat and looked at my surroundings. To me, my new home was a dream come true; I literally felt, and still feel, like a princess in her castle! I have my independence, space and privacy, yet just across the road is a whole row of houses occupied by families who know me and love me and who are available to help me anytime should the need arise.

I started work on the first of July 2012. My working hours are generally from 09:00 to 13:00, though, if necessary, I will stay at work longer. What an absolute pleasure not to have to be up at the crack of dawn in order to be ready and at work at 07:00. I usually get up around 07:30, spend some time in the Word and then get ready for work, which is within walking distance, so I often walk to work just so that I can get a bit of exercise!

At first, we were not really sure what I would be doing at the church office, but as time has gone by, I have found my little niche. One could say that I am more into the communication side of the ministry. For instance, I do the monthly calendar, CD ministry and part of my job is to upload the sermons as well as other pertinent information onto the church website. I am also involved in the ordering of groceries for the Seminary hostel. I often help out with PowerPoint slideshows for various pastors!

This relaxed work environment has truly had a wonderful impact on my well-being. I love my job and I feel so very blessed to be working where I am living.

I no longer feel such anxiety at the first signs of illness because I know that, if necessary, I have the freedom to stay in bed and recover without fretting about losing my job. This peace in itself makes a very big difference to my recovery.

My feline family

During one of our visits to the flat prior to moving in, Bev and I looked out of my window and saw a beautiful cat. It was grey, with white paws and a cute little white face and its grey tail had a white tip. Though it was a feral, I knew that cat would become part of my home.

Quite quickly after moving into my flat, I was frequently visited by two ferals. One was the grey cat and the other was a skinny, shiny black little cat with bright green eyes. They were very wild though very curious about the new resident in their territory. Despite Shirley's protests, I began putting food out for these two. Shirley did not want to see me experiencing the heartache of losing another pet. But I just could not ignore those two pairs of big green eyes looking at me full of expectancy every day. And yes, very soon these two ferals had names: "Smokey" and "Velvet".

Smokey and Velvet were extremely wild, never daring to cross the threshold of the doorway into my flat. Any sudden movement and they would scatter. Feeding them outside became a daily routine.

I was flabbergasted one morning about a month after moving in as I looked out and counted seven cats around the feeding bowls. Though these cats looked well cared for, I wondered what I had gotten myself into. A couple of days later I was very distressed as I looked out and saw Smokey acting very strangely. I was sure she was experiencing something like a fit, but moments later everything made sense. Smokey was a female and Smokey was in heat. All the courteous visitors now made sense. I was soon to find out that Velvet too was pregnant.

I monitored the mothers closely and when they had given birth, I found their dens and watched them from a distance until the kittens were three weeks old. Rosemary had become very good friends with me and often visited me while I was staying in Matt and Elizabeth's house. She was in her seventies and lived at an old age home and she too loved cats. With the help of Rosemary, her daughter Rolene and a whole lot of drama, we managed to get all six kittens and their wild Mums into my bathroom. For an entire month, I had eight cats in my bathroom. Thankfully, there was another bathroom adjacent to my flat which I used during that period. At the time. Rosemary still had her car and faithfully came every day to help me clean sandboxes, feed and care for the cats.

I had always wanted a long-haired tortoiseshell and one day, while sitting and watching the kittens, I mentioned this to Rosemary and in unison, we both looked at one of the kittens which was mottled and had long hair. She was affectionately known as little "Fluff Ball" and I realized that she was meant to belong to me. I instantly had a name for her: I called her "Chelsea" as she had all the colours of a Chelsea bun. Chelsea was so fluffy that from behind it looked as if she was wearing baggy pyjamas, so her nickname became "Chelsea Bum".

We managed to find homes for the kittens and Rosemary and I were very tearful as we parted with them. Before finally releasing the two mother cats from the bathroom, we had one more thing to do. They needed to be sterilized. The task was daunting, but once again Rolene kindly came to our rescue. Early one morning, after a bit of wrestling, Rolene managed to get the Mums into cat boxes and Rosemary kindly took them in to be sterilized. Being feral cats, the vet very kindly performed the operations for me at a very discounted price.

My mission had been accomplished, with the amazing help of Rosemary and Rolene: I had managed to prevent the church property from becoming overrun by feral cats. Now I had a family of three cats who continued to keep the church mouse population down. Chelsea was a great source of joy and entertainment, while Smokey and Velvet continued to keep their distance. However, at this point they were more comfortable coming indoors for their food and eventually Smokey frequently slept on the bed, although she would not allow me to touch her. It was two years from when I started working with the two ferals before I could actually stroke Smokey and even then, it was only on her terms. Strangely enough, our special time of affection would be in the mornings, in the bathroom of all places, while I was getting ready. I would have thought that after a month of confinement in the bathroom, it would be the one place that she would avoid. Amazingly, she would become so loving, brushing up against my legs, flopping down and rolling over like a little kitten. Her purr was deep and loud and only occasionally would she let me stroke her.

Sadly, in September of 2014, Smokey was hit and killed by a car on the busy road that runs past my flat. I was heartbroken. It has now been six years since I started working with Velvet and she has become a real little house cat. One would never say that she was once completely wild.

Chelsea is well known on the church grounds. She loves the gardeners and follows them around all day. On Sundays, she loves going around and greeting people at their cars as they arrive for the church service.

My secret garden

Though I had been attending the church for many years, I am sure that, like many, I had never realised what existed beyond the seminary hostel building one sees as one drives through the gates into the secure parking area of the church. Beyond the hostel building was an area filled with shrubs, bushes and beautiful trees. This area would one day be my garden. I have always loved plants and gardens. Ever since I can remember, I have dreamt of owning my own. So, from the first time I looked through the sliding doors of my flat and saw the little front garden filled with shrubs, bushes and beautiful trees, my mind could not help but wonder about the potentials that the little garden had to offer. I would often allow my mind to explore those potentials and I would envisage beautiful flower beds and a lush green lawn, perhaps even an outside garden suite.

Once I had settled in, I asked Ian if he would mind if I did what I wanted in the garden, especially as it was out of sight and not much use to anyone else. Ian graciously gave me the go-ahead; it was like letting a child loose in a candy store.

Over the years that I have been living in the flat, that little garden filled with shrubs, bushes and beautiful trees has been transformed into a beautiful, flourishing garden with a lovely lush lawn and pretty flower beds. The uneven ground leading out into the garden has been levelled and paved, with even a path winding through the garden, wide enough for me to use with my motorised wheelchair. A lapa was built especially for me, and I enjoy many summer evenings and Saturdays outside. I also have a magnificent water feature that provides me with great enjoyment and relaxation. The wonderful development of this garden and all its features is a combination of the generosity and incredible labour of love of so many dear friends. Tucked away out of sight, it is a perfect little haven for me to sit, spend time with my Lord and relax and enjoy the outdoors in the comfort of a wicker couch.

The blessing of where the Lord has me now in my life is often too overwhelming for me to comprehend. Way back, while still living within the choking walls of Green Acres, never did I ever think that I would one day be living on my own in such a lovely flat with my own beautiful garden. Back when I was living and working at the school, surrounded by the continuous, overwhelming, humming noise of four thousand children, facing the daily challenge of trying to cope in an extremely intense work environment along with trying to deal with weakening health, never in my wildest dreams did I imagine that I would end up in a situation where I am living totally independently in such a peaceful environment, surrounded by such great love of neighbours who are just so available and eager to assist wherever and whenever necessary.

Keep your lives free from the love of money and be content with what you have, because God has said, "Never will I leave you; never will I forsake you."

— Hebrews 13:5

151

Chapter Twelve:
Snake in the Grass

For our struggle is not against flesh and blood, but against the rulers, against the authorities, against the powers of this dark world and against the spiritual forces of evil in the heavenly realms.

— Ephesians 6:12

An eagle has excellent eyesight. It can see from afar its enemies, such as snakes, trying to sneak into its nest to steal its egg or to kill its young. Though eagles build their nests on high rocky places, snakes have a tendency and ability to climb them. But the strong vision of eagles, more often than not, keeps the enemies away from their nest.

The year 2015 started off with great excitement! Samaria Mission is a faith mission, working from the platform of Christ Baptist Church. Samaria Mission desires to be obedient to the Great Commission by effectively becoming involved in the process of church planting through evangelism, discipleship, church development and social upliftment. Most of their work is done in and around Mozambique! During a specific time of the year, they have what they call "outreach season". This is a season when Samaria Mission staff takes numerous short-term teams into Mozambique to serve in various villages for an average of 10 days per team! Most of the teams come out to serve from America. However, there are a couple of South African teams that also go on these trips, one being from Christ Baptist Church, my church.

The teams stay in tents, use long drops and makeshift showers. With no electricity, cooking is done with gas and a generator which runs from 06:00 to 10:00, lighting up the camp at night.

Going on an outreach trip had always been a dream of mine; a dream which I didn't believe could ever be realized due to my limitations. Over the years that I had been staying in my flat at the church, I had become good friends with Mark and Alicia Raley who are neighbours of mine. Being involved in their lives, I was aware of the mission trips they would go on. I would so enjoy listening to the feedback and hearing how God was not only working in the lives of the villagers but especially in their own lives. I loved watching their faith grow and seeing their excitement each time they returned from an outreach.

The Raleys would often invite me along with them but I didn't think I would cope. I knew that the mission staff would have to make special adjustments to make it possible for me to go and so my pride got in the way and I would always find an excuse not to go.

Finally, over our Thanksgiving meal in 2014, I made up my mind that in 2015 I would go on an outreach to Mozambique. Mark and Alicia knew me well and I knew that they would not lead me into situations where I could not cope.

I experienced God's Hand of Provision from the time that I decided that I would be going. I did exceptionally well in my network marketing business and as the Lord brought people along my path who needed help, I was able to accumulate enough commission to pay for my trip and even to pay for necessities for the trip.

The build-up to our trip in June was thrilling; the unknown was almost overwhelming. The Raleys were away in the States but as Brad and Sharyn answered and provided solutions to each nagging question that I had regarding camp life, I became more excited and convinced that this would be a trip of a lifetime.

The sole purpose of these outreaches is to share the gospel with the unreached, the unreached whose lives revolve around witchcraft and ancestral worship. So, in preparation, we are reminded that we are about to enter a spiritual warzone and we are cautioned to expect more trials than usual, before, during and after an outreach. *"For our struggle is not against flesh and blood, but against the rulers, against the authorities, against the powers of this dark world and against the spiritual forces of evil in the heavenly realms."* Ephesians 6:12. We are encouraged to have at least three people commit to intercede for us during this period. I did not realise how vital this intercession would prove to be and I am so grateful for the people who faithfully prayed for me. A month before the trip, I experienced unusually intense muscular pain. At times, I even found it too painful to walk. Though we couldn't quite figure out the cause, I was kindly given weekly massages; they were painful but extremely helpful.

The Monday before we were due to leave, I was munching a bag of crisps and I ended up choking on a crisp, I felt it go into my right lung (my weak lung). The next day I went to see the Doctor as I was coughing badly and I could feel that the crisp was still lodged in my lung. I was concerned that it would cause an infection. Much to my horror, my doctor was seriously discussing the possibility of a hospital stay; the crisp had to be removed. Many heartfelt prayers went up to my heavenly Father whilst waiting in the consulting room. I just could not miss the outreach. After consulting with a specialist, my doctor concluded that the crisp would eventually dissolve and a hospital visit was not necessary. On our way back to the car, I managed a deep cough, and praise God, the crisp dislodged. I was filled with awe and thankfulness. However, as a result of the injury to the lung, I was very ill and ended up spending three days in bed. Though coughing and voiceless, I was in the car at 05:30 on that Sunday the 28th of June 2015, leaving with the team for Mozambique. I knew that I was taking a risk; my doctor had warned me about the risk of pneumonia but I knew that so many people were praying for me. I was also certain the warmer weather in Mozambique could only help the healing process.

It was really sad that the Raleys were not able to be with us on my first outreach due to visa issues. However, we were still in really good hands with Brad and Member who are both staff members of Samaria Mission.

Our goal for going on outreach is to encourage the local church and reach the unreached with the gospel but little did I know that the Lord had a few appointments with me.

The first day in camp was very overwhelming for me. There was just so much happening around me and my normal everyday routine was non-existent. Because of very unfamiliar surroundings, much to my irritation, I found that I needed much more assistance than usual. As is so habitual for me, I found myself racking my brains trying to figure out ways to do the things that I was battling with on my own. But the Lord, in His gentle way, showed me that in my pride, I was robbing others of blessing by not allowing them to help me. By His grace I was able to let go, and, not too long into the outreach, I was asking for help and fellow teammates were happy to give it, never thinking less of me. This is but one of the many lessons the Lord taught me during the outreach.

Most mornings, I went along with the other ladies on hut-to-hut visitations. Because the sand outside the camp was so thick, we had to use the manual wheelchair which was really difficult to push through the sand. I loved hut-to-hut visitations; I loved being in the village, and, on two occasions, I was privileged enough to witness two ladies confess Christ as their Lord and Saviour.

Though nervous, I got to teach the ladies twice during afternoon ministries and it was during this time that I rediscovered my love for teaching God's Word. The first day that I taught it felt as if the ladies were not retaining anything. Later, we realized that their focus had been on the Cerebral Palsy (it was probably something very new to them). However, my second day of teaching went extremely well by God's amazing grace. I had such fun interacting with the ladies and the women even gave me the Shangaan name "Mikateko" which means "Blessing". I was also grateful for the wonderful bond that was built between Jane (the interpreter) and myself. Contrary to what we had expected, Jane had no difficulty in understanding my speech; this in itself showed God's power in action.

We serve an Almighty Lord and whatever barriers remained concerning the villagers and my disability came down on the Wednesday night when I gave my testimony during the evening service. It was a wonderful privilege for me to share. Though what I shared was about the incredible works that He has done and continues to do in my life, without Him I am nothing. I was completely speechless the next afternoon when, during the ladies' ministry, one of the ladies presented me with a brand new sarong. A sarong is a large colourful piece of material worn by the ladies to cover their legs. In this culture, women must cover their legs when in the presence of other men. As a sign of respect to their culture, all the women on outreach teams wear sarongs during ministry. To these people, a new sarong is very expensive and represents great value. It was an incredibly humbling experience for me to accept this gift from these precious ladies, knowing that back at home I have wardrobes full of clothes, more than any of these ladies owned.

One morning, I went along to where the well was being drilled and spent the morning watching the final stages of the well being assembled. I found the process fascinating and much to my joy, when it had been completely assembled, I had the privilege of pumping the first water from this well.

Another morning, the team stayed in camp and helped put new thatching on the church roof. What a joy it was for me to see the villagers and team members working side by side, chatting and laughing despite the language barrier, the common thread being the Joy of the Lord. Oh, make no mistake, I managed to get myself lovely and dusty as I helped carry bundles of thatch with my electric wheelchair.

Though camp life was not always easy, whatever pain experienced from sleeping on a stretcher, fatigue, no matter what the discomfort, all challenges and discomfort faded in comparison to the absolute joy experienced of being out in Mozambique with people who live in absolute poverty. For me, this setting is a harsh reminder of how my priorities so easily become out of line with what is important to our Lord. The people of Mozambique have nothing but out of their poverty, they still give with joy. These people live from day to day, making the most of each day.

Most of all, I am so incredibly thankful to the Lord Jesus Christ. He had so much more in store for me personally than reaching out to others. He brought healing to wounds that I had thought had healed long ago, but, in reality, they were still very raw and festering, even preventing me from serving Him the way I should have been serving Him. I praise Him for sustaining me through each busy day; this in itself was amazing as I usually tire easily, and most days back at home, I have to take a nap in the afternoons. Most of all, I praise Him for reigniting my first love, my love for my Lord and my Saviour, Jesus Christ.

A Day on Outreach in Mozambique

Days on outreach are very full.

The day starts at 07:30 with coffee and morning devotion. After breakfast at 08:00, the ladies are divided into small groups and each group goes into the village on hut-to-hut visitations with an interpreter to share the gospel! It is always exciting to find that as we go from hut to hut throughout the week, there is a clear understanding of the lessons that are being taught during the afternoon ministries!

The men usually remain in camp doing physical work like drilling wells or building churches.

During the afternoons, from 14:00 until after 16:00, we have men's, women's and children's ministries!

At 19:00 pm, we have a service preached by one of the camp leaders. What a joy it is to watch close to over 50 men, women and children come from the village through the darkness. After a wonderful time of worship and dancing, they sit on a tarpaulin under a floodlight, which is run off a generator. Before the preaching, one or two of the team members get the opportunity to share his/her testimonies.

After the evening service, we all gather together in the kitchen tent for "wrap up" where we report on the day's ministries, praising the Lord for the work that He is doing in the lives of His people, over a mug of hot chocolate before heading for bed. I praise God for the Samaria Mission team and the incredibly hard work they put into making these trips possible! I thank God that they make it possible for ordinary church members to experience the joy of mission work!

Since my first mission trip to Mozambique in 2015, I have been privileged to go on three other trips to Mozambique in 2016, 2017 and 2018. Each trip that I have gone on has been full of such enriching and life-changing experiences.

The battle is lost but the war is won

Dad had been the level-headed one in the family. He was always on top of the finances. He always planned ahead. He could sense trouble and steer the family away from it to the best of his ability. He always pushed Cristo and me to overcome whatever challenges we faced. He supported most of my endeavours. However, Dad and I were very much alike in many ways and this often caused us to clash, but it was not long before we made peace! My dad was my hero, and, as with most daughters, almost everything I achieved was to make him proud!

Due to the poor economy, in 2005, Dad found himself without a job. However, he had a great knowledge of mechanics. He had rebuilt a number of vehicles from scrap, among others a Ford F250 and a Chev Nomad! Dad was a jack of all trades and master of all. So, he started working for himself, fixing and maintaining vehicles and farm implements for farmers in the community.

Working for oneself has its own set of challenges. As the economy worsened and more farms were being sold to the government, Dad's customers became fewer and fewer. In time, the month-end became a nightmare for Dad! He had to pay 6 people's monthly salaries but the income he was getting was often barely enough to cover even these! Dad found himself using his credit card to pay salaries, not to mention other monthly expenses. This was not in Dad's nature; he hated debt but before he knew it, he was in over his head! Stress and influential "friends" caused him to find escape in alcohol. For a while... his stress dissipated!

Over a period of ten years, I watched my dad change for the worse! It became more and more difficult to have a simple conversation with him without it being blown completely out of context. Eventually, Dad and I barely knew each other. Being the one living with Dad, it was my mum who suffered the most during this time! Mum's love for and dedication to Dad never wavered, however, and Dad was never physically abusive.

In late 2013, Dad became very ill, showing signs of liver failure. His doctor sternly advised him to stop drinking! For a period, Dad did cut down and started to show some signs of recovery. But, as the financial stress continued to worsen, Dad again found his escape in alcohol!

In May 2015, Dad was in great discomfort and his doctor realized that his abdomen was enlarged. This enlargement was due to ascites, a process where fluid fills the abdomen as a consequence of a failing liver. The doctor tried to perform a paracentesis, to drain this fluid from the abdomen. It is a very dangerous procedure, where only 500ml of liquid can be drained at one time or the body goes into shock.

Realizing that his health was in serious trouble, Dad amazingly made the decision to stop drinking completely that May and he never looked back. I was so proud of him. He was a completely different person. He became the dad and husband that we had known and missed. It was wonderful having him back. It was wonderful to sit and have a decent conversation without worrying that Dad would take things the wrong way.

At the end of June that year, I was going on my first outreach trip to Mozambique. My parents were so excited about my trip that Dad went out and purchased a very special camping chair for me. This chair was not sunk in like the normal camping chairs, making it easier for me to get in and out of. It also has a collapsible table attached to the side of it. This chair was not cheap but Dad was determined to get it for me as he realised just how significant this trip was to me.

The house in which my parents had been living was sold and the new owner gave my parents only two weeks to move out! My parents had nowhere to go and the stress on them was tremendous. The new owner had wanted the house for his son. He insisted that the five-year rental contract which my parents had was not legally binding. My dad did not have the funds to dispute the issue in court. Eventually, the previous owner of the house kindly said that my parents could move into his farmhouse. His family had moved into town and so he was hardly ever there. In his garden was a little cottage, into which he kindly moved for the nights that he did stay on the farm. Packing up and moving out of a house in which you have lived for eight years is no easy task, let alone having to do it in just two weeks!

Upon my return from my first outreach, I received word that Dad was not doing well. The stress and the intense heavy lifting from the move had taken their toll. Dad's abdomen had become very swollen and uncomfortable. Despite his discomfort, he pushed himself as far as he could to try and get the new home in order, replacing geysers, hanging pictures, connecting appliances and so much more. His abdomen continued to swell and no matter how many water pills the doctor prescribed, his condition just kept getting worse.

In early August, I accompanied Dad when he went for a sonar of his liver. Mum had to work and I did not want him to go alone. The doctor performing the sonar was unknown to us. After examining Dad's liver, he callously patted Dad on the shoulder and told him that his liver was so shrivelled up that it was beyond repair. He told Dad that he did not have long to live and then he left the room. I went into the bathroom at the hospital and cried; I so desperately wanted to be strong for Dad but I was crushed by what I had just heard. Dad had chronic liver cirrhosis.

Liver cirrhosis is when scar tissue replaces healthy liver tissue. This stops the liver from working normally.

The liver has many important functions including:
- Removing waste from the body, such as toxins
- Medicines
- Making bile to help digest food
- Storing sugar that the body uses for energy
- Making new proteins

My precious friend Liz had sat me down and explained to me the course of chronic liver cirrhosis. What I was hearing was unbearably painful, though, in time, I was incredibly grateful to Liz for bravely preparing me for what lay ahead.

Over the next month, I got a lift home to Tzaneen every weekend with a dentist who worked in Polokwane and lived in Tzaneen. I am so thankful that I had these weekends with my parents. We spent time together, talking, laughing and making new memories. Each time I went home, I saw how Dad's condition was worsening. It broke my heart and I was determined to be at home with them as often as possible. I knew deep down that I needed to make the most of these visits… The church was very gracious and gave me time off work, especially when my lift to Tzaneen left on a Thursday afternoon and not a Friday. However, I always tried to ensure that my work for the week was up to date.

My parents and I had always clashed when it came to the topic of religion. At one stage, it was so bad that I refused to even mention it at home. Mum and Dad had grown up in the church and what they were seeing in me was completely different to what they knew. I had become "born again" at the age of 17 and they had a different understanding of this. To be "born again" is the simple act of confessing Christ as Lord of our lives and believing in our hearts that He rose from the dead. And in doing this, we are saved!!! Romans 10:9 *"If you declare with your mouth, "Jesus is Lord," and believe in your heart that God raised him from the dead, you will be saved."* Being concerned parents, they had been worried that I had fallen prey to some kind of cult.

God's timing is not our timing; I had tried so many times over the years to explain to my parents what the true meaning of being "born again" was but it only led to conflict! One weekend at home, after my trip to Mozambique, I took out the evangie chart which we use in Mozambique to share the gospel.

The "evangie chart" is an A4 flip chart which I had made from using the pictures of the commonly known evangie cube. I found it difficult to use the cube as it is small and difficult for me to work with. I needed something that I could use without struggle. I needed to be able to give my full attention to lovingly and prayerfully giving the Gospel. I printed each picture of the evangie cube in size A4, laminated and ring-bound the pages in the correct order. This was not only extremely helpful to me but we soon realised that the elderly people with poor eyesight in the villages were able to see the pictures more clearly and understand better. The "evangie chart" also proved to be a very helpful tool to other members of the mission team. Eventually the chart was printed in size A3 and handed out to all the pastors in various villages of Mozambique by Samaria Mission staff who shepherded and held these pastors accountable. You are welcome to see how the "evangie chart" is used on YouTube at https://youtu.be/JWDvA0KUzU8

Back home with Mum and Dad I demonstrated how we had used the chart, sharing the gospel with them as I had done in Mozambique; I prayed that they would finally understand that having grown up in a church does not automatically make us Christians. It is only by acknowledging that we are wretched sinners in need of a Saviour that makes us Christians. The Lord spoke to Dad that Sunday, and, much to my joy, Dad asked me to pray with him that night. From that night, we prayed together every night when I was home. Over the weekends that followed, I watched Dad become a completely different person. He seemed to be at such peace. He noticed and appreciated the little things in life. He was truly joyful in spite of everything.

Dad's swelling was increasing daily as the liver's daily functions continued to fail. No matter how many water tablets the doctor prescribed, the swelling just worsened. Dad's legs were so swollen that moisture would seep through any weak spot in his skin and run down his legs. He was so uncomfortable.

At this stage, Dad was incapable of continuing with his business and the only meagre income they had was from Mum's administrative job at the local trading centre.

The doctor tried once more to perform a paracentesis on Dad but the wound from the incision had continued to seep during the night and the doctor decided that the procedure was just too dangerous to try again.

Dad was taking handfuls of tablets three times a day! Mum and I pumped him full of all sorts of home remedies. Although I had been told by experts in Mannatech that the products would not help reverse chronic liver cirrhosis, I stubbornly insisted on making sure Dad got in as much of the products as possible. Dad was so positive, faithfully consistent in taking his medication.

Dad was losing muscle mass, as his body could no longer metabolise proteins in his diet. Despite this, I was determined to ensure that he remained well-nourished.

We planned a family get together for Dad's 63rd birthday. Cristo and Lee came up from Richard's Bay. I was worried about my brother and the shock he would experience when he saw how ill Dad was looking. Cristo and Lee were extremely alarmed when they saw Dad upon their arrival on the farm but managed to conceal their shock. Dad requested my special chocolate cake! We celebrated   Dad's birthday on the Saturday afternoon when Cristo and

Lee arrived (4 days before Dad's actual birthday)! Dad was thrilled to have his family with him and the afternoon was a happy one. Through that Saturday night, Dad did not feel at all well and we worried that the cake had been too rich for him, especially as he had insisted on having two pieces!

On the Sunday morning, Dad was extremely weak. However, he insisted that we go to church as a family and Cristo had to help him into the vehicle. Dad had a renewed understanding of communion and he wanted us all to have communion together as a family; this was his wish even though everyone could see how weak he was.

Dad had made his famous oxtail for Sunday lunch the day before and after church, Mum finished cooking it for him. He only managed a few mouthfuls and went to lie down.

I was due to go back to Polokwane early that Monday morning but by 20:00 that Sunday night, I had made the decision to cancel my lift back and stay at home. Dad was extremely restless during that night and by early Monday morning he was completely disorientated. Dad's doctor kindly came out to the farm in the morning but by that time Dad had slipped into a hepatic coma. A normal functioning liver metabolizes and detoxifies substances formed in the body during digestion. Inflammation, infection or damage to the liver causes toxins, like ammonia, which is formed when digesting protein, fatty acids, phenol and other toxins to be released into the blood, crossing the blood-brain barrier, negatively affecting the central nervous system, leading to a hepatic coma.

This is what happened to Dad. Apart from keeping him sedated, the doctor informed us that there was nothing more that could be done for Dad. Though I had known deep down that the end was near, we were all devastated. I was so grateful that Liz had taken the time to explain to me what to expect because it helped me understand what was happening to Dad but it by no means made it any easier.

The doctor gave us the option of putting Dad in hospital (50km away). Mum refused and we all decided to keep him at home where he would be surrounded by people who loved him dearly. Thankfully, Lee had some background in nursing and so the doctor left her with injections to give Dad every 6 hours to keep him sedated.

My aunt Caroline and uncle Henry (Dad's brother) had come through from Machadodorp (3 hours away).

Late that Monday afternoon, before his next injection, Dad showed signs that he was aware of his surroundings. Again, God's timing was amazing because at that time Dad's pastor was ministering to him and I could see that Dad had a good understanding of what was being said to him. My aunt and uncle were also able to have a conversation with him. Though he could not speak, we could see that he could hear and comprehend us. From then on, he deteriorated rapidly and by morning we were praying that the Lord would take him Home. Dad was using every muscle in his body just to take a breath. None of us will ever forget how he suffered. The Lord took him Home just before 10:00 on Tuesday the 1st of September (one day before his 63rd birthday).

The reason that I am writing about Dad in such detail is by no means to shame him but to honour him. He had turned to alcohol as an escape from financial stress. But he had completely turned his life around and had found true joy despite financial stress and failing health. Though he had lost the battle with liver failure, he had found his Saviour and through Christ, he had won the war and now enjoys eternal life with the Father! Knowing Dad, he would have wanted his story to be told in the hope that it would help prevent somebody else from suffering the same fate. *"But encourage one another daily, as long as it is called "Today," so that none of you may be hardened by sin's deceitfulness."* Hebrews 3:13

Dad's salvation is an incredible gift to us! Having full assurance that he is indeed with His Saviour is what has comforted me through the devastating time of losing my precious father. I know that I will see him again!

The Christian battle is real. Like the sharp-eyed eagle who can spot its enemy from very far distances, our eyes need to be alert, always on our Saviour and Protector. As we fix our eyes on the world, the danger of being overcome and broken by trials in this world is also very real because that is exactly what the enemy wants.

> *And pray in the Spirit on all occasions with all kinds of prayers and requests. With this in mind, be alert and always keep on praying for all the Lord's people.*
>
> **— Ephesians 6:18**

Chapter Thirteen:
The Battle Is Taken to New Heights

So do not fear, for I am with you; do not be dismayed, for I am your God. I will strengthen you and help you; I will uphold you with my righteous right hand.

— Isaiah 41:10

Snakes are part of an eagle's diet. The eagle has a unique way of conquering its prey! The eagle does not fight the snake on the ground. It picks it up and takes it up into the sky, changing the battleground.

In the air, the snake has no stamina, no power and no balance. It is useless, weak and vulnerable, unlike on the ground where it is powerful, wise and deadly.

The New Normal

The loss of my dad was devastating. I just couldn't believe he was gone. Going around town with Mum, Cristo and Lee finalizing funeral plans was just so hard, as we watched other people just going on with their everyday lives. *"Did nobody realize that such an incredible man, husband and father was no longer with us here on earth?"*

Life without Dad changed everything! Dad was the linchpin of the family. He was the glue that held everything together in the family. Without him, going through his paperwork, trying to figure out insurances and finances was incredibly difficult. Dad was the one who handled everything!

The person most affected was Mum. Mum's entire world had revolved around Dad and after forty-two years of marriage, she didn't know otherwise. To make things worse, the day after Dad passed away, Mum was callously informed by her boss that she no longer had a job!

Thankfully, Dad had a few insurances. One paid out without any questions and we were so grateful. The other one, however, paid the first amount owing towards the funeral. Two weeks after my dad had passed away, however, this insurance company sent out one of its agents to interrogate us! My mother had driven around for two hours trying to find him and bring him back to the farm as he had gotten lost. This gentleman spent two hours making us relive every part of Dad's death. Even though we both eventually broke down in tears, the gentleman persisted with his heart-wrenching questions, taking advantage of our vulnerability. He did not hesitate to go through personal files, taking photos of important personal documents. What a violation of our privacy!

Needless to say, this insurance company refused to pay out the outstanding balance of the policy on the weak grounds that Dad had omitted to answer three pathetic questions correctly upon taking out the policy telephonically. The company had faithfully deducted their monthly premiums, and, only after a claim was submitted did they decide to investigate the legitimacy of the policy. I tried my best to fight this company with the help of a friend who is a lawyer but sadly I did not have the funds to take the company to court.

Mum was devastated! Within a period of two months, she had lost her home, her husband and her job!!!

The church very kindly gave me a few extra weeks of compassionate leave so that I could finish going through Dad's paperwork and just be there for Mum.

It broke my heart to leave my mum alone on the farm when I eventually went back to work for the first time after Dad's passing! We were incredibly blessed in that the owner of the house kindly allowed Mum to continue living in his house rent-free. It really was kind of him! Mum also had incredible neighbours who were always there for her when she needed them. Mum and Dad's church family also provided Mum with great support. However, Mum was still living alone in a large farmhouse. Security around the house was very good and Mum had her dogs.   Still, knowing that she was on her own was a great concern, especially as farm attacks are so prevalent in South Africa.

Mum agreed to let me oversee her finances. This was something Dad had always done. Mum found herself overspending partly because she was not used to budgeting but also because of the need to fill the void left by Dad. We knew that the little money she had would have to last her for the rest of her life. Eventually, I obtained permission from Mum to manage her finances. Mum had so little and somehow, we needed to ensure that it lasted.

Mum was living on a very tight budget. The only income she had was the State pension and a small monthly amount from Dad's insurance which she had invested.   She had four dogs and three cats to feed. Fuel costs were very high as the nearest town was over fifty kilometres away.

I lived three hours away and it wasn't always easy to go and visit Mum. When I did get to see her, looking into her eyes was like looking into an empty shell. Mum neglected herself, partly due to finances but mostly because her way of life had changed so drastically; she was grieving and trying to adapt to her new normal way of life. Dad was no longer around to do odd jobs around the house or maintain the vehicles and Mum had to learn to ask other people for help.   After forty-two years of living with her soulmate, this was, and still is, a huge adjustment.

Four months after Dad died, the farm was sold, though the new owner kindly assured Mum that her home was secure! Sadly, nine months later, Mum was informed that her house was needed and she had two months to find another home and leave!

Cristo and Lee were preparing to emigrate to New Zealand and they wanted Mum to live in their house in Richard's Bay (nine hours away from me). This would have been ideal in many ways but I was not at all happy with Mum being so far away! Mum could not physically or financially afford to frequently travel so far to visit me. I was also concerned that there would be nobody to keep an eye on her, make sure she was eating properly, etcetera.

Mum is very family orientated; she needs to have family around her! It was bad enough that Cristo and Lee were emigrating but I simply hated the fact that Mum would be so far away as well. This was an incredibly worrying time. Mum refused to come and live in Polokwane.

Eventually, in the November of 2016, after Mum had been told that her house was needed, aunt Caroline and uncle Henry very kindly proposed that Mum should move in with them. My uncle and cousin Tony worked incredibly hard during the following couple of months in order to convert the back part of their house into a flat for my mum. The flat is beautiful and spacious, just perfect for Mum.

Sadly, before Mum could move, she had to have her four dogs and three cats put down. They had been part of the family for so many years and Dad had loved his cats, but we had no choice. Nobody wanted to adopt old animals and even if someone did, Mum would not have agreed to it without being completely assured that her animals would receive the same love and affection that they had become so accustomed to.

Lizzie, Mum's wonderful friend and neighbour, made it possible for the vet to come through to the farm. Uncle Henry and Tony drove through to be with Mum. I just couldn't be there; I knew that it would be too upsetting for me and I did not want to put myself at risk of another fall. Apart from losing Dad, having her animals put down was one of the most heart-wrenching things Mum had ever had to do. Thankfully, the vet was very sensitive to the situation and she made sure that this terrible ordeal was quick and painless!

Mum has settled in very nicely with my aunt, uncle and Tony. She is so happy in her little flat. It is so much better than living alone in such a big farmhouse. Mum and my aunt get along so well and though Mum is independent in her flat, she is seen as part of the family and is always included in family outings, etcetera.

The drastic improvement in Mum's circumstances has had a great impact on my physical well-being even though she is living further away from me! It is scary how stress can translate to one's physical state. Amazingly, I find that I am more stable on my feet, simply because I am not constantly worrying about Mum. I have peace of mind and can concentrate more on my walking. I am truly grateful to my aunt and uncle for taking my precious Mum in.

The fall

At 12:00 on the 25th of December 2015, I woke up to find the Christmas tree lights still on, my battery-operated candles still flickering and my television still blaring. I had unintentionally fallen asleep on top of my silky bed cover in my silky nightgown. As I got up, still sleepy, my mind was not only filled with what needed to be switched off etcetera but my heart was filled with great sadness at the thought that this would be the first Christmas without Dad. Mum had gone down to Richard's Bay to spend Christmas with Cristo and Lee. I had chosen to stay at home; I just wanted to be alone, so concentrating on getting off the bed safely did not even feature.

Before I knew it, my feet had slipped out from under me and I had slid off the bed and landed on my right side on the floor. Somewhere on my way down, I had heard a loud snap. My left arm was in pain and I guessed that I had broken it, though being my only functioning arm, I prayed that it had only dislocated.

I lay on the carpet for an hour, struggling to get myself up. However, as I lay there, I experienced a deep sense of God's peace. Since Dad's death in September, I was not only filled with grief but had been so busy trying to help

Mum, deal with the estate and fight insurance companies. In short, I was so busy chasing my own tail that my relationship with the Lord hardly existed. Lying on the carpet, I knew without a doubt that my Lord had an appointment with me. He had taken the time to throw me a curveball. I knew that I was about to embark on a journey that would redirect my focus back to Him and change my life. I felt incredibly loved by my Lord. *"For thus says the One who is high and lifted up, who inhabits eternity, whose name is Holy: "I dwell in the high and holy place, and also with him who is of a contrite and lowly spirit, to revive the spirit of the lowly, and to revive the heart of the contrite."* Isaiah 57:15

Eventually, I managed to curl my feet around the legs of my bedside table and use my stomach muscles to pull myself up into a sitting position. From there, I was able to pull my cell phone off the bed and call the Raleys, amazingly using my "useless" right hand to make the call. The Raley family are one of the families who live close by and who have a set of keys to my flat. Just five days before, Mark had suggested that Alicia put my cell number into her "favourites" on her phone, that way even if the phone is in "sleep mode", if I call, the phone will ring.

Mark answered the phone at 01:00 with a very cheerful, Texan accent; *"Merry Christmas, Debbie,"* but upon realising that I was in trouble, it only took them a couple of minutes to get over to my flat.

Mark and Alicia took me to the hospital. Initially, I was strong; perhaps it was the adrenaline but I hardly felt the pain. I broke down when X-rays showed that my humerus had fractured badly and that I needed a plate and screws. I was devastated! Such a bad break to my precious left arm meant that my independence was at risk. For the rest of that night and into the following day, I purposed to take every thought captive, refusing to allow fear of what the future could hold to overtake me. *Finally, brothers and sisters, whatever is true, whatever is noble, whatever is right, whatever is pure, whatever is lovely, whatever is admirable—if anything is excellent or praiseworthy—think about such things.* Philippians 4:8.

By 03:00, I had been booked into the hospital and scheduled to be operated on in the morning. I was eventually wheeled into the theatre holding room with Mark and Alicia beside me at around 02:00 on Christmas Day. The Raleys had brought a couple of Christmas gifts that had been under my tree in my flat for me to open. I was extremely uncomfortable because I had been lying in the same position since I had been admitted the night before. Changing position required the use of my left arm, which was broken, and it was difficult for others to help me. There was much laughter as I tried to open the gifts with my "useless" right hand.

Two hours later, on my way back from the theatre, still groggy, I was overwhelmed to find Alicia waiting for me in my ward. I felt extremely loved. The operation had gone well and I came out with a plate and eight screws in my arm.

I stayed in the hospital for four nights. The nurses couldn't seem to grasp the fact that my left arm was broken, my right arm is non-functional and that I actually needed feeding, etcetera. I had a wonderful team of church family who took turns at mealtimes to visit and feed me.

For the first month after my operation, I stayed with Basil and Annette, very close friends of mine. This family embraced me as one of their own. Annette, being a qualified nurse, was able to give me the nursing I needed during the early days after my operation. I was completely dependent on her for everything from simply getting up off the bed, bathing, brushing my teeth, feeding; literally everything. The only thing I could do was sit in a comfy chair with my tablet and the Word of God (turning the page simply by swiping the screen, was an accomplishment in itself). This, however, was exactly where I needed to be, spending hours in His Word and in prayer.

I could not even check my emails, couldn't follow up on Dad's estate, and couldn't check up on Mum and her finances. All I could do was sit at the feet of Jesus. Though this was a time of anguish, great uncertainty about the future, having to swallow my pride and accept help from everyone around me, it was a time of rest and a time of sweet fellowship with my Lord. It was a time that I would not exchange for anything in the world.

Every day was a celebration as pieces of my independence slowly returned to me. It is amazing how we take for granted the simple act of getting up off the bed, the joyful privilege of dressing oneself, the privacy of being able to use the bathroom independently!

The bone in my arm had healed well but the radial nerve was bruised when I fell and, as a result, I had a "drop wrist" which meant that I had no wrist function and very little finger function in my left hand. Recovery of the nerve was an extremely slow process and therapists even expressed concern that the nerve would not recover. Once again, I had to discipline my thoughts because if I had allowed them to run away, I would have gone mad. If the nerve did not recover, I would lose my independence and have to go back into the home and stay there for the rest of my life. I knew deep down that the Lord would give me the ability to accept this unimaginable outcome if that was what He wanted for my life, but until such time, I resolved to not give up trying to persevere with my daily home therapy, believing that our Lord would restore the nerve damage!

I experienced the Lord's incredible providence through my Specialist, Physiotherapist (Matt & Elizabeth) and Occupational Therapist. They all kindly insisted on seeing me on a regular basis, completely free of charge. I saw the Lord's kindness through various people in the church who selflessly transported me to my appointments.

In late January, I became part of the Raley family. I stayed with them for four months. Although, in the beginning, I was still very dependent, I was yet again made to feel part of the family. The Raley house is spacious and was perfect for me to be able to get around in my electric wheelchair on days when I was particularly tired. Mark and Luke (their son) took the time to build a ramp at the kitchen door so that I could get in and out of the house with my electric wheelchair. Mark also put a rail in the shower so that eventually I would be able to shower independently. Alicia was very sensitive to my needs and was always available to help, though she knew that the ultimate goal for me was to regain my independence and move back into my flat! She did whatever she could to help enable me to accomplish more and more on my own. Every "small" accomplishment like brushing my own hair or starting to dress myself more and more was a victory, a celebration.

My Orthopaedic Surgeon recommended that I wear a dynamic splint. *This is a splint using springs or elastic bands that aids in movements initiated by the patient by controlling the plane and range of motion.*

This would help keep muscles in my wrist and fingers active and prevent the shortening of ligaments due to lack of use while the nerve was healing! The splint was custom-made by the Occupational Therapist who also recommended that I wore a different splint at night! This splint was more like a "static" splint which ensured that my wrist and fingers remained outstretched and prevented from curling inward during the night. This too was custom-made!

Mark took charge of my home therapy which included electrode treatment every evening. We all, including Luke, had many moments of great laughter during therapy time, moments of absolute joy when we saw the slightest signs of wrist movement. We also had times of despondency and disappointment when it seemed as if there was no improvement. But those times pushed us all back to our knees in prayer and reminded us that God is Sovereign, His timing is not ours, His Will is not always our will but His promise to never leave us is sure.

I was also very privileged to spend every second weekend with Shirley and Seth! We spent great times of fellowship on their veranda! Seth and Shirley, as well as so many others, were so supportive, they rejoiced with me over "small" achievements and encouraged me to improvise and try different ways of doing things such as use my "useless" right hand to feed myself. This was a messy endeavour, but, with extreme effort, a victorious one!

At times, I become impatient, wanting my recovery to speed up so that I could get back to full independence but I realized that my time with the Raley family was a very special gift from the Lord. I truly enjoyed the experience of being part of a loving God-fearing family and it was my prayer that He would use me in their lives as much as He used this family in my life. Sometime at the beginning of March, I received a surprise email from my very close teenage friend, Brett! He had emigrated to Australia and had a lovely wife and two beautiful young girls. Brett had written to tell me that he would be visiting South Africa and was planning to come up to Polokwane to see me! I was beside myself with excitement. I had not seen Brett in over 20 years and he was planning to make the three-hour journey just to come and see me! The visit became even more exciting when I heard that Darrell would be coming too. There was, however, one problem, Brett and Darrell's visit coincided with a very special church family wedding that I had been invited to. I had two options - either cancel that very special visit and go to the wedding or excuse myself from the wedding and spend my time with my brothers from my teenage years. I went for option number three and asked the bride and her groom if they would mind having two more guests at their wedding, guests that they did not even know. They kindly agreed, and, much to everyone's surprise, I arrived at the wedding flanked by two very good-looking men that nobody at the wedding knew, except me! My reunion with Brett and Darrell was so incredibly special; though twenty years had gone by since we had last seen each other, it felt as no time had passed at all. The three of us had such a wonderful evening together. Both took turns in feeding me without batting an eyelid. To top it all, Brett and I surprised everyone by taking to the dance floor! Almost everyone at the wedding knew me very well, especially as it was a big family church wedding but very few knew that I could dance! That evening was one that I will never forget! God's timing is so spot-on; He knew that this special visit was just what I needed at that exact time!

Though recovery felt extremely slow, six weekly visits to my Orthopaedic Surgeon revealed that there was definite improvement; the nerve was slowly but surely recovering. The joy and relief were overwhelming! I had returned to work in late February. In the beginning, I found it extremely difficult to operate the computer, not to mention controlling the mouse. Wearing the dynamic splint did not help as my fingers were confined but by God's grace, and with intense concentration, my work was always accomplished.

As recovery to my radial nerve became more apparent, my Surgeon suggested that the splint be adapted. Instead of all my fingers being confined, an elasticised "pulley" for each finger was attached to the splint, making it possible to use each finger individually and making it easier for me to type and regain more of my independence.

By April, though slower than usual, I was doing almost everything on my own and we began making plans for me to move back into my flat.

Rosemary had very kindly and unselfishly moved into my flat since the 25th of December, the day of my fall, and had faithfully taken care of my feline family. I began spending afternoons after work in my flat and Rosemary would help me go through drawers getting rid of junk! I sold my bedroom suite; it included a headboard, two bedside tables and a dressing table with many drawers! The bedroom suite was precious to me as it was older than I was and it had belonged to my parents. The tough decision to sell it had to be made; it was taking up too much space in the flat! The goal was to make the flat safer for me and the more space I had meant the less there was to fall over!

My dear friend Brett and his brother-in-law kindly blessed me with the funds needed to make the flat even more "Debbie-proof" and members of my Bible Study put up rails in my shower and at the entrance to my flat. Because I now had so much more space in my flat, Annette and Basil blessed me with the comfy chair in which I sat while I lived with them for the first month after my operation. This chair has been such a blessing. Instead of sitting uncomfortably on the bed to read or watch television at risk of falling asleep unintentionally again, I now enjoy my comfy chair.

So many people were involved in helping to make my flat safe enough for me to move back! Their support and determination to help me continue enjoying my independent lifestyle is truly overwhelming, a true demonstration of family in Christ!

Finally, after much planning and preparation, I moved back into my flat in the middle of May. At first, it was strange being back on my own in the flat, especially as I had become so used to having people around me. However, with all the changes that had been made to the flat, it was like moving into a new home and of course I thoroughly enjoyed being with my feline family again. My wrist had not yet fully recovered and I still had "butter fingers", dropping most of what I tried to pick up. Mark had spent much time searching for a hands-free kettle where I could just place my cup under the nozzle, switch a knob and boiling water would fill my mug. A couple of days before leaving the Raley home, Mark, Alicia and Luke presented me with a huge box. Inside was the perfect hands-free kettle. I would not have to lift a kettle of boiling water with the risk of pouring boiling water all over myself; what an incredible blessing!

Being on my own in the beginning made me a little nervous and cautious about trying to do too much and falling again. However, I continued with my home therapy and I continued to see improvement.

My nerve has made a full recovery. Much to the surprise and joy of all my therapists, I can fully extend my wrist; what an incredible blessing. Even over two years later, at times, I still lie in bed and extend my wrist just because I can. I never want to take such a simple yet vital movement for granted!

God's fingerprints

Before my fall in December 2015, I was working hard with my editors to have this book finally published. I had not written about the passing of my dad as that was still too raw at the time. After my fall and during my recovery, my editors urged me to write about my dad as this would bring my story full circle, from being totally dependent on my parents to becoming self-supportive and then to being a support to my mother in various ways. *"Oh, and while I was writing, I could just as well write about my fall,"* they said. At my recovery rate, I wondered if this book would ever be published.

In November 2016, I took two weeks' leave to go and visit my precious friend Liz in Johannesburg as I had not seen her in such a long time! The main purpose of the visit, though, was to finally finish this book. Liz had a beautiful little cosy home! I hadn't seen Charlie dog in three years, and being extremely protective and possessive over Liz, we were not sure how he would cope. Much to our surprise, he remembered me and rarely left my side for days. It was a very special reunion. Liz's front yard was so spacious and green! It overlooked a plot that was filled with peacocks and rabbits.

Most of my hand function had returned. I had planned and set goals for each day towards the completion of my manuscript and Liz faithfully held me accountable to those goals, making sure that coffee, water and all sorts were always available to keep me going. In the evenings, Liz and I would sit on her veranda with our coffee, throwing balls for the dogs and watching the sun go down, chatting and laughing. It was wonderful to be together again. Being a doctor, she not only understands me as a close friend but she also understands the implications of someone with severe Cerebral Palsy! Often, after a day in front of the laptop, Liz would take out her dry needling kit and needle all the knots that had accumulated in my neck and shoulders as a result of sitting hunched over the laptop all day!

I was really surprised at how well the writing had gone; the manuscript had been completed ahead of time! Liz was overjoyed and she made a special dinner in celebration of the completion of my book after so many years of working on it! However, the reality did not sink in for me. I couldn't shake the feeling that this manuscript was not complete; something did not feel right. Liz and I spent the rest of my visit walking through the big shopping malls of Johannesburg or just chilling! Though I had done much work, my two weeks with Liz were truly a blessing from the Lord, a carefree holiday full of laughter! Exactly what the Doctor ordered after the events of the past fifteen months!

At the end of my time with Liz, I got a ride back to Polokwane with close friends. It was a Saturday when I got home. Once again, Rosemary had stayed in my flat while I was away! Apart from giving me peace of mind by looking after my cats, for Rosemary, being at the flat is more central for her! She has no need to find a lift to church, her very close friends live just next door and the shopping mall is closer for her! Being a Saturday, Rosemary decided to spend the night in one of the hostel rooms as there were no students that weekend and so she would not have to find a lift to church the next day! Having Rosemary spend the night meant that we could catch up and enjoy some fellowship together! At this point, please bear in mind that every moment of our lives has been orchestrated by our Heavenly Father! *"Your eyes saw my unformed body; all the days ordained for me were written in your book before one of them came to be."* Psalm 139:16 Thankfully, I had done a bit of unpacking before I went to sleep that night as I did not want to fall over bags that were lying around!

I was woken at around two that morning. My Ginger cat (another stray cat who had found his way into my heart) was leopard-crawling over my face; he was spooked! I felt as if I was drugged but I wanted to check on Ginger. As I looked up from my bed through the darkness, I saw the silhouette of a person in my room. I thought nothing of it. Knowing that Rosemary does not always sleep through the night, I thought that she had snuck in to make herself some coffee. I called out her name but she did not answer. Instead, I watched as this person picked up my handbag. Still thinking it was Rosemary, perhaps sleepwalking, I called louder and proceeded to get out of bed and put the light on. The silhouette moved into the kitchen and as I was trying to get up off the bed, I saw the flicker of a flashlight in the kitchen. I wondered why Rosemary was not responding to my calls! I reached my main door which Rosemary would have used to come in and found that it was locked. *Something was very strange*. I looked into the kitchen and Rosemary was not there. Reality hit me like a thunderbolt, and, as I pulled the curtain away from the kitchen window, I saw that the burglar bars had been cut. I had just been burgled.

I searched for my cell phone to call for help and realised that it had been stolen. I screamed at the top of my voice for Rosemary, asking her to bring her cell phone, and as I waited for her, the reality of what had been stolen began to sink in. My precious laptop, my handbag and my tablet were all gone. My first real panic was that not only my bank cards were gone but more importantly, my mother's bank remote was gone; I was almost beside myself. *"What if they found a way to hack into Mum's bank account and take the little money she had?"*

The next heart-stopping thought that crossed my mind was my manuscript. We didn't have Wi-Fi at Liz's place so I couldn't back up my final chapter into the cloud; however, I did make backups onto two memory sticks and kept them in my handbag, separate from my laptop. My laptop had been stolen and the fleeting comfort I felt from knowing I had backups disappeared as I remembered that the memory sticks had been in my handbag and my handbag was gone.

Rosemary and I finally managed to get hold of Pastor Johann who lives just across the road. He was with us in no time and called the police for us. We had called the police around 03:00 am; they only arrived at 09:00 am, six hours later. While waiting for the police, Pastor Johann walked the perimeter of the church grounds and not far from my kitchen window, just outside the room where Rosemary had been sleeping, is an alcove where the students are able to sit and enjoy fellowship. In this alcove, he found my empty laptop case and my handbag which had been turned inside out and all the contents were strewn all over the floor. The robber kindly left my purse with my Identity Document and all my bank cards; he had just taken the cash out of the purse. By God's amazing grace, he had also left my mother's banking remote. Much to my absolute horror, the only things he took from my handbag were the two memory sticks!

181

The sticks had been safely placed in an inside pocket of the handbag with Mum's banking remote. He had rummaged through everything so fast, between the time I had realised that I had been robbed and the time I shouted for Rosemary. He could have actually still been in the alcove when Rosemary came out of her room. I praise God that she was not hurt. *"Why had he specifically taken my memory sticks and left Mum's banking remote which looks very much like a memory stick?"*

I was so incredibly thankful that we had found my Identity Documents, bank cards and especially my Mum's bank remote. Words cannot express how devastated I was that I had lost all the work I had put into completing my book. That loss far outweighed the loss of my cell phone, laptop and tablet all put together. Make no mistake; these devices are vital to me, especially my laptop, as I rely on it so heavily due to my inability to write. But the last chapter of my book was gone! I just couldn't believe it; all that hard work was just gone! I drove around the block in my wheelchair countless times, just praying that the thief had dropped one of the memory sticks. Even church family walked around looking and praying that they would find one of my sticks with the backup but to no avail.

I know that all things good or bad work together for the good of those who love Him and I had a very strong sense that there was more to this than just a robbery.

The police came and took statements and forensics came to lift fingerprints but could only lift one clear print. We could see where he had climbed the back wall and left his muddy footprints but that didn't help the investigation.

Thank the Lord I had household insurance and after submitting all necessary documents and police reports, I received a payout much higher than I had expected. This not only enabled me to replace my devices but to get devices of high quality so they would last. My old laptop was ten years old and I know that if I look after my new one, it too will last me ten years, if not more.

The church kindly enhanced my security by installing Maxiwindows on the large windows in the kitchen and bedroom. Jeff, a good friend from the States, kindly funded the installation of a Maxiwindow in my bathroom as well as a Maxigate at the entrance to my flat. I marvel at God's providence.

Though I still could not figure out why that last chapter had disappeared, at times, I wondered if the Lord even wanted the book published at all, but the urge to rewrite and finish the book never went away. The Lord has blessed me with such a wonderfully fulfilled life despite all odds, so how can I not share it with others and give Him the glory?

My second attempt at finalizing this book has been so much more productive! In retrospect, I realise that the first attempt had been written in anger. "*If Dad had not let go of himself, he would still be with us. He would not have passed away, we would not have suffered such grief and I possibly would not have had such a serious fall and taken so long to recover!!!*"

I was still grieving and did not know how to write about Dad's passing in a way that would honour my father and bring glory to God! Make no mistake; the first attempt was by no means a waste. The first attempt was almost like a cleansing process for me! It helped me face and process head-on the fact that my dad was gone from this earth. In fact, the evening of the day I had initially written about Dad at Liz's place, I was so physically ill that Liz had to help me into bed.

This is why I am convinced that God's fingerprints were all over the robbery. If Rosemary had not spent the night, I would not have had any way to call for help. Neither Rosemary nor I were hurt in any way. My old devices were replaced with brand new ones which I would never have been able to afford with my own finances. Who knows, perhaps the robber would end up reading my manuscript and end up coming to Christ. The point is; it was not God's will for that last chapter to be published the way it had initially been written.

The past two years have been extremely difficult. The pain of losing dad has, at times, been unbearable! Breaking my arm and the fear of losing my independence resulted in times when I wanted to give up and I begged the Lord to take me home. The frustration of being robbed and losing that last chapter, (all that hard work) almost resulted in me giving up on publishing this book. The purpose of this book is solely to bring Glory to God for the incredibly fulfilled life that I am privileged to lead despite all odds.

Throughout this time, my Lord has turned my face from my circumstances upwards and helped me focus my eyes on Him. As with the eagle with its snake, if he doesn't lift it off the ground into the sky rendering it useless, the snake will overcome the eagle! So, we need Christ and His Word to help us stay focused on Him instead of being overcome by our circumstances.

> *"Whoever dwells in the shelter of the Most High will rest in the shadow of the Almighty. I will say of the LORD, "He is my refuge and my fortress, my God, in whom I trust." Surely he will save you from the fowler's snare and from the deadly pestilence. He will cover you with his feathers, and under his wings you will find refuge; his faithfulness will be your shield and rampart."*

> — Psalm 91:1-4

Conclusion:
Wind Beneath My Wings

He will cover you with his feathers, and under his wings you will find refuge; his faithfulness will be your shield and rampart.

— Psalm 91:4

I am so very thankful for the challenging chapters which the Lord has taken me through in my life. Had I not gone through them, I would not appreciate what I now have. I would probably not even have been sufficiently equipped to cope on my own as independently as I do.

I chose the imagery of an eagle because of my great love for eagles; the African Fish Eagle, in particular, depicts so perfectly how God always faithfully and lovingly carries His loved ones through the highs and lows of life.

God uses much the same kind of principle in our lives: if we expect to live happy prosperous lives, free from hardship and trial, the only people we are fooling is ourselves. The trials (thorns) in our lives are so necessary because God uses them to get us out of our worldly comfort zones. And as our focus is turned towards God, we long for eternity. When those of us who are in Christ leave this world of trial and hardship, we enter into the magnificent presence of the Almighty God and receive brand new glorified bodies free from all pain and suffering! As Christians, our trials serve as a reminder to us that this world is not our home.

Contrary to the common belief that if one does not receive physical healing here in this life one is spiritually lacking, Paul actually boasted in his affliction. *"Three times I pleaded with the Lord to take it away from me. But he said to me, 'My grace is sufficient for you, for my power is made perfect in weakness.' Therefore I will boast all the more gladly about my weaknesses, so that Christ's power may rest on me."* 2 Corinthians 12:8-10

Paul's eyes were focused more on bringing Christ honour and glory while he was on this earth. He knew that the joy and honour of bringing glory to his Lord, coupled with experiencing a deeper relationship through his total dependence on the Lord, far outweighed any fleeting relief from earthly discomfort.

In no way do I claim to have arrived. There are so many areas in my life where I still need to grow and mature. I continue to rely on His strength to help me through each and every day. Trials, and especially temptations, continue coming my way and for as long as I am on this earth, I will always face them. As turbulences in the air, they are ever-present, causing me to slow down and ponder the status of my relationship with my Lord.

Knowing Jesus and the price He paid on the cross for my sins, which enables me to enjoy direct access to the Father, is what makes every muscle spasm, every daily struggle, every physical fall, every hurdle, every patronizing comment from people who are none the wiser, so worthwhile. I find my comfort and strength in the knowledge that I was bought with a price that was paid once and for all. I know that every day of my life was written before one of them came to be. I know that He knit me together in my mother's womb; my physical disability was no mistake. What a joy and an honour it is for me to know that as long as I am here on earth, He is using me for His glory. What an incredible joy it is for me to know that there is great purpose in everything I face. What great peace I have in knowing that when I die, not only will I receive a new and perfect body, but I will be with Christ for eternity!

Dear reader, do you know Jesus? Do you know the price He paid for you?

Do you know that your life has invaluable meaning and great purpose? It is only in Christ that you can find such great purpose, peace and contentment in a world filled with such turmoil, ultimately free from the fear of death. All that is necessary is that you trust in Him as your Lord and Saviour. He knows your heart and your thoughts and He hears the prayer of a repentant heart. It is as simple as Romans 10:9:

> [11]*"If you declare with your mouth, "Jesus is Lord," and believe in your heart that God raised him from the dead, you will be saved. for with the heart one believes and is justified, and with the mouth one confesses and is saved. For the Scripture says, "Everyone who believes in him will not be put to shame."*

> *Therefore, since we have been justified through faith, we have peace with God through our Lord Jesus Christ, through whom we have gained access by faith into this grace in which we now stand. And we boast in the hope of the glory of God. Not only so, but we also glory in our sufferings, because we know that suffering produces perseverance; perseverance, character; and character, hope. And hope does not put us to shame, because God's love has been poured out into our hearts through the Holy Spirit, who has been given to us.*

> **— Romans 5:1-5**

Lightning Source UK Ltd.
Milton Keynes UK
UKHW020931301121
394812UK00006B/80